GREEN GAST

GREEN GASTRONOMY

A Fresh Way of Eating

COLIN SPENCER

BLOOMSBURY

Plate sections: page 1 © Alan Newnham, pages 2, 4, © Anthony Blake;
pages 3, 5 © Merchurst; page 6 © Alain Proust; page 7 © Tim Hill;
page 8 © Charlie Stebbings. Page 6 picture supplied by Cephas.
All others supplied by Anthony Blake photo library.

The information in this book was correct to the best of the editor's and publisher's
belief at the time of going to press. While no responsibility can be accepted for
errors and omissions, the editor and publisher would welcome corrections and
suggestions for material to include in subsequent editions of this book.

This edition first published in 1996 by
Bloomsbury Publishing plc
2 Soho Square
London, W1V 6HB

Copyright © by Colin Spencer 1996

The moral right of the author has been asserted

A copy of the CIP entry for this book is available from the British Library

ISBN 0 7475 2298 7

10 9 8 7 6 5 4 3 2 1

Designed by AB3
Typeset by Hewer Text Composition Services, Edinburgh
Printed and bound in Great Britain
by Clays Ltd, St Ives plc

CONTENTS

———

WINTER MAIN DISHES

WINTER SIDE DISHES

WINTER PUDDINGS

SPRING

SPRING SOUPS

SPRING SALADS

SPRING MAIN DISHES

SPRING SIDE DISHES

SPRING DESSERTS

SUMMER

SUMMER SOUPS

SUMMER SALADS

SUMMER MAIN COURSES

SUMMER SIDE DISHES

SUMMER PUDDINGS

AUTUMN

AUTUMN SOUPS

AUTUMN SALADS

FOREWORD

T his book is about eating well, eating with style, with an emphasis on freshness and rich, intense flavours. The food described has been influenced by many factors which are coming to fruition, so it is food for the coming age, when environmental and social pressures will make us all change our diet.

It has been claimed that good cooking derives from an intimate relationship between the land and the kitchen. This relationship has been weakened and almost destroyed by sophisticated technology, intensive cultivation boosted by large amounts of chemicals, modern processing and patterns of world food distribution. But it is this relationship that this book aims to reconstruct. The modern, over-refined diet with its high amounts of saturated fats, salt and sugars promotes big bones, height and greater body weight, as well as the diseases that the affluent West is prone to. What we need now is a diet that promotes brain tissue and stimulates intelligence as well as general health, but which also recognises the effects it has upon developing countries and the environment itself. Such a diet exists, and if we believe in the future of humanity, this is our only hope for the future.

Thus, a new form of gastronomy has been called into being by necessity. This way of eating produces gourmet meals without any animal products, and I swear its recipes are as mouth-watering and delicious as any other revered cuisine.

Until very recently meals composed of dishes like those in this book were thought most odd. But times are changing. Society is more fluid. People don't think in such hard and fast ways any more. Many of the recipes are mainstream dishes served in élitist restaurants, where chefs might be surprised to know that they also happen to be politically correct. In my view this makes their flavour all the richer and more satisfying.

If we can struggle to remove all the old hang-ups about an animal-free diet and think of it as the new green gastronomy full of inviting food, we will find at a stroke that the food becomes far more beguiling and palatable. Such is the power of thought: the attraction of a food lies in our perception of it. I fervently hope that these pages might help to change and correct the unfair public perception of this way of eating and that the recipes may ensnare the taste-buds even of those with the most entrenched beliefs in orthodox gastronomy.

MAKING A
STATEMENT

Friends and colleagues, all with a great and genuine love of food, have been somewhat alienated by my recent espousal of the plant diet. 'What on earth do you eat?' they cry in disbelief. When I tell them (and these pages are full of the recipes) they look disgruntled, as if no respected food writer should be allowed to omit from his diet such traditional delicacies as unpasteurised cheese and butter, crème fraîche and caviare, and a hundred other appetising products and flavours. Well, I have and I feel great. 'Clean' is the word that comes to mind. A feeling of lightness too, as if one has suddenly begun to draw in lungfuls of mountain air after being trapped in the pollution of a great urban centre.

I have always had a passion for strong and intense flavours, so in this new diet I decided to intensify the flavours and to widen their range. I have used combinations of herbs, spices and ingredients I would not have dreamt of before. As a result, I don't believe there is a moment of dullness, nor lack of stimulation in my daily diet; rather, it proves to me time and time again that you gain immeasurably from omitting many products and striving to find appealing variations in those that are left. In doing so you are making a statement about your own relationship with the world, a statement in my view that is profoundly worth making.

Note Various serious issues which surround the plant diet are discussed in the Appendices at the end of the book.

WHAT MAKES
A CUISINE?

Why should French or Chinese cuisine be praised as food fit for gourmets while British cooking be spurned? Climate has a lot to do with
it, as the strength of the sun and the length of daylight increases
the range of vegetables and intensifies their flavour. But as our climate
gets warmer we should be cultivating more and more Mediterranean vegetables.

Tradition also plays another strong part in this value judgement of na-
tional cuisine. But if tradition means a past history of cultural ideas built
up around the cultivation of food plants, the gathering of indigenous wild
plants, the hunting of local game, the rearing of livestock and the preparation and cooking of these ingredients in recipes which are passed on from
generation to generation, and which change, are adapted and go on growing with new ideas, surely the British should have a cuisine as well as
anyone else? They should, but I believe that the Enclosures Acts, which
deprived landworkers of both common land and the means by which
they grazed their livestock over a period of 100 years throughout the
eighteenth century, destroyed all the traditions we once had. For when
farmworkers left to join the new boom towns of the Industrial Revolu-
tion in middle England, they left behind the land and the animals and
even the means by which they made fires to cook with. Recipes which
had been passed from mother to daughter were suddenly not made any
more. The food they now lived on (and a very poor diet it was – tea,
bread, cheese, sugar and a bit of bacon) were all shop-bought. In my
view, the greatness of British cooking has been lost to us for nearly 300
years.

Apart from tradition, what are the other elements that turn an area's
cooking style into a cuisine? The ingredients themselves are often particu-
larised by the area, such as the white truffles of Bologna, or the climate
might make one food product more favoured than another, such as the
beetroots of eastern Europe. Local herbs will also be used to flavour recipes in a particular way (parsley sauce is a famous English accompani-
ment). Quite often cooking receptacles will differ too, their shape having
come about from the demands of a fire (the paella dishes of Spain), the time

needed to cook the dish (the hanging cauldrons of the Middle Ages) or the material at hand (terracotta dishes of the Mediterranean).

I have explored this subject in some detail because I see no reason why, in time, the plant diet or animal-free cooking should not also be thought of as one of the great cuisines. In my opinion it is already great. From across the world we already have some of the finest vegetable dishes that go back centuries: the pasta dishes of Italy, the vegetable gratins of France, the green curries and spicy noodle dishes of the Far East, the wonderful vegetable curries of southern India, the beetroot soups of the Balkans and Russia, the tabboulehs of the Middle East, the couscous of north America, the salsas and cornbreads of Mexico and South America. Remember that the greatest dishes, and the tastiest, always come from the poorest parts of the world. If you have no money and precious little to eat, you have to stick to grains and vegetables, but by God you make them different every day with spices, herbs and flavourings, often picked from the wild and costing nothing. It is the rich who borrow from the traditions of the poor, but they never improve a dish by their changes: they usually soften the intensity of flavour and thereby dissipate its integrity.

The majority of people throughout history have lived on a simple plant diet which has been highly seasoned and flavoured by the herbs and spices at hand. Often their seasoning, such as the soy sauce of the Orient and the tomato sauce of Italy, have been taken up with enthusiasm by omnivores. The plant diet has always had its own particular foods, which food technology has now made available to us all: a great range of seaweeds and soya products, from cream and milk to tofu, tempeh and miso; spices such as lemon grass, galingale and ginger; various types of chilli; and a year-round supply of garlic. My cooking tends to borrow from everything that is good and tasty. Like British cooking today, it is eclectic, borrowing from all countries at all times, merging one style with another. It certainly has its own particular flavours, sometimes veering towards the oriental in its use of lime and ginger, sometimes towards the Americas in its use of chilli, sweetcorn and maple syrup, and sometimes to Europe in its use of garlic, basil, root vegetables and rosemary.

The style of a meal owes much more to the East than to Europe, being comprised of many small dishes rather than a single large one accompanied by two smaller ones. Consequently, the four seasons in this book have each been divided into five sections: soups, salads, main dishes, side dishes and puddings. A meal might very well comprise a soup and three side dishes, or two salads and a main dish, depending on the season and one's appetite. Puddings are not *de rigueur*, but as cheese is entirely omitted and the last course, or penultimate course in France, does not feature, puddings, if you have the room, are a pleasant way of concluding the meal.

SO WHAT DO YOU EAT?

———

I n a perfect world, home-grown organic vegetables would be the norm. Most of us, however, live in great urban centres and are forced to buy our food from supermarkets where the vegetables have often flown many thousands of miles before arriving on the shelves. If you have the chance, buy from market stalls (the produce may not look in such prime condition but has been proved to be fresher and certainly cheaper) or farm shops, the next best place to your own garden, where you know the produce has been grown locally. Not only will the vegetables taste better, their vitamin and mineral content will be higher.

Buying good bread is something of a headache: the public seems to have formed a taste for dough which is pumped full of air and water and which tastes of packing foam. Health and wholefood shops now stock a range of dense, chewy bread, much of it organic, all of it wholegrain, which is nutritionally valuable, highly satisfying and worth every penny it costs. Of course, you can also make your own bread, which can be pleasurable and fulfilling, or madly irritating and disappointing, depending on one's nature, skill and experience. I give no recipes here, for I lack patience and confess that my bread-making is a spasmodic affair. Also, as I never follow a recipe and cannot stop adding herbs and flavourings, my success rate is fairly low. However, there are excellent manuals on bread-making if you wish to try your hand.[1]

Much plant cuisine can be eaten raw. In fact, for health and good digestion I would recommend a daily dish of raw grated vegetables or a salad of green leaves. Nuts, seeds or chopped dried fruit can be added to salads for extra taste and texture. I am also very fond of warm wilted salads, which count as raw, for the leaves or vegetables are hardly cooked at all, merely seared for a brief moment. One of the greatest taste sensations is where a vegetable remains succulent and almost raw inside, but its outside edges have been seared under such heat that the sugars have caramelised and the exterior has just slightly blackened. Be generous with the flavours of garlic, chilli and ginger and use the very best extra virgin olive oil.

SOYA PRODUCTS

———

Much of the plant cuisine rests on that miraculous ingredient the soy bean. Modern technology can turn this major world crop into all sorts of fantastic food for animals and humankind. Soy sauce is one of the strongest and finest of all flavourings, but remember that it is also a food, high in nutrients. Invest only in very good soy sauce and have both light and dark varieties at hand. I do not use tofu much at all, for I cannot say I am greatly fond of it; it is too bland by far for my palate. The only way I like it is when dipped in a strongly spiced batter and deep-fried. The crisp, highly flavoured exterior is a wonderful contrast to the milky centre. Tempeh, on the other hand, is highly flavoured; some people liken it to a ripe and smelly Brie. It can be bought frozen in most wholefood shops and will keep happily in your home freezer until you want to use it. Thaw it out, slice it into chunks about 2.5cm/1 inch square and fry in olive oil with garlic and ginger until brown and crisp on the outside. This is also good mixed with potato and onion.

When I first became vegetarian almost twenty years ago, products like soya mince and chunks were very nasty and I eschewed them completely. Besides, who wanted a meal composed of a substitute meat with two veg on the side, exactly the kind of plateful I had expressed disgust for? The world, however, has moved on: technology's and people's taste-buds have been refined and there are now a few substitute meat products on the market which are really very pleasant. Go out and experiment with them to see what you like. If you want such dishes, you can buy readymade shepherd's pie and *chilli con carne*, both *sans carne*, and tasty enough, I wager, to fool any omnivore. I have given no recipes for such dishes because it was not in the remit of this book. Simply follow traditional recipes and substitute soy as a protein for the meat. (You will find that soya mince needs hardly any cooking at all, so the finished dish is often much easier and quicker to make.)

A product about which I am really enthusiastic is soya cream, which I use extensively in both savoury and sweet dishes, cooked and uncooked. I also use soya milk in certain soups and other recipes. The great advantage of soya milk and cream is that their fat content is very low, but they do include protein and carbohydrate. I enjoy their flavour, rich but not fatty. When cooked, soya cream can give body to a tart or roulade so that, once cooled, it will hold together when sliced.

STORE
CUPBOARD

——

Experiment with flavoured oils and vinegars of which there are now many varieties: raspberry and sherry vinegar, balsamic vinegar, good-quality red and white wine vinegar, and cider vinegar, which is good for everyday use. Herb vinegars can easily be made at home by placing a sprig of rosemary, a few cloves of garlic, a chilli or whatever you fancy in a bottle of cider vinegar and leaving it to marinate for a few weeks. Take out and discard the flavouring ingredient before it makes the vinegar musty.

Always have extra virgin olive oil for use on salads and vegetables, but for cooking use virgin olive oil. Walnut and hazelnut oils are also good for some salads. For oriental dishes use peanut, sunflower or sesame oil. Buy good-quality soy sauce and use Maldon sea salt and freshly ground black peppercorns. Always have a good-quality Dijon mustard at hand, and some mustard powder to make up your own. Make your own curry powder and garam masala from freshly roasted spices.[2] Find out where your nearest ethnic stores are; Indian and Chinese food shops are now widely distributed in the UK, but if you have trouble getting to them, some do an excellent mail-order service.

In spring and summer try to grow your own herbs, even if only in a window-box. Basil, chives, parsley, thyme, sage and tarragon can all be grown easily enough and are better than dried herbs, which soon lose their pungency and should be thrown away if their aroma has lessened. Keep bottles of rosewater and orange flower water in the pantry. Hang up dried chillies, onions and garlic, and keep a small stock of shallots and lemons.

Tins of tomatoes are always useful, as is a tube of tomato purée, and tins of haricot or flageolet beans are handy for making a quick supper. A jar of sun-dried tomatoes in oil or in a packet are invaluable, as are packets of dried porcini or oyster mushrooms. If you are lucky enough to find a glut of mushrooms or fungii in the autumn, dry them for future use by spreading them on newspaper over a dry, gentle heat such a radiator, boiler or Aga.

Useful spices from the Orient include ginger root and lemon grass. The first keeps well and needs peeling, then finely slicing, but if it gets too dry, throw it away. The second loses its pungency quickly and should be used a few days after being bought. Galingale, another root, has a wonderfully aromatic flavour and should also be used quite quickly: prepare it like ginger. Try more oriental condiments such as nori and soy sauce (a black, intensely flavoured purée), wasabi (a stingingly hot form of horseradish), amchoor (dried mango in powdered form) and tamarind (sold either as pulp or paste). Asafoetida also loses its pungency with age, for which some people will be thankful: when new, its smell and flavour are immensely powerful and can be nauseating; when old, its garlicky aroma is appealing and its flavour in a dish often lifts it to realms of intense savouriness.

EQUIPMENT

———

A wok is very useful, for at its simplest, plant cuisine can be a few mixed vegetables, prepared and sliced, then stir-fried with a drop of sesame oil, a little garlic, ginger and chilli, and sprinkled with a little salt, sugar and lime, or soy sauce or dry sherry. Such a dish could be a meal in itself, its impact depending on using the freshest vegetables available. Of all the woks I have tried over the years I have now found what I consider the best, which is an electric one. This quickly gives a very high heat, and comes with a lid so that you can partially steam the vegetables too. It also has an internal rack so that vegetables which are partially cooked can sit on it for a moment to continue steaming. This wok also makes the most delicious fried rice: you need only about 5ml/1 tsp of oil and the rice will crisp and brown without burning or sticking.

A fairly powerful blender is probably the most used piece of equipment in my kitchen; it is invaluable for making soups and purées. I find I do not use the larger and more complicated food processor as frequently, though the grating disc on it is vital for making winter salads.

Strong, cast-iron saucepans with thick bottoms are also invaluable, for many of the recipes in this book use no added water when cooking vegetables – they simply sweat in their own juices. This technique ensures maximum flavour, and a strong, thick-bottomed saucepan allows you to do this without the vegetables burning. A large copper frying pan is also useful, as copper heats up fast and ensures a greater heat than most other substances, cutting down the cooking time.

A triple steamer, electric or otherwise, is necessary, especially for cooking new potatoes with mint. Other essentials include a collection of wooden spoons, a set of very sharp knives, good thick chopping boards and a clear, uncluttered work surface. The preparation of food before cooking is highly important if you want good results in a finished dish.

THE ULTIMATE SLIMMING DIET

——

I have never met an obese person upon this diet, though it is possible to meet fat vegetarians as their diet can be too high in cheese and dairy products. However, even a person who omits all animal produce could suffer from clogged arteries with a diet high in avocado and coconut milk, although this is not likely unless you live in the South Pacific.

Anyone changing over to this way of eating will see a steady weight loss, especially in the first three months, until the optimum weight is reached, when the weight will stabilise. My own weight loss was as small as 1 kg/ 2lb a week, but it was constant and continued for about four months. But what is even better news is that a change to the plant diet, with its high amount of fresh fruit and vegetables rich in anti-oxidants, will clear the arteries of saturated fat deposits. Anyone doing so will feel younger and greatly more energetic, for you are as young as your arteries.

CHANGING OVER

———

If you are really convinced that the plant diet is the right diet for you, all will be pleasurable and a huge relief. If you're not convinced, then you have not really committed yourself and it is probably best to go slowly, cutting down on dairy produce rather than giving it up altogether, and trying non-dairy meals two or three times a week. You will be surprised how you don't miss those fatty ingredients and find after a few such meals how much lighter your body feels and how much energy you have. Your body is your friend: it will enjoy being treated well and will respond accordingly.

If, as an experiment, you want to try the diet for, say, a period of three weeks, you will be amazed at the difference. Human metabolism is a miraculous chemical structure which is made to adapt. Every species is geared to survive and we are no different. Within a short time your body will lose all yearnings for the foods you have omitted, be they cheese, milk or bacon. In fact, within a few months it will send signals of disgust to your brain at the smell or sight of such foods.

In the beginning it might be a wise idea to start treating yourself with various foods which are special favourites. There are amazingly good soya ice-creams, for example, and you can make excellent fruit sorbets from your favourite berries (see the recipes on pages 54 and 84). Experiment with many of the strange but highly exciting oriental flavourings that ethnic stores stock. Try some of the ready-made dishes to see if there are any you like, and don't forget to test the meat substitutes just to see whether any are tasty enough to satisfy. In the end I think you will conclude that nothing can beat really tasty home cooking, that the ready-made dishes leave much to be desired, their range of flavours being too timid and orthodox and the portions far too small. Besides, home cooking takes very little time. A simple dish takes no longer to prepare than opening a packet or tin and sticking it in the microwave. It's also fun, which is what life and eating is all about.

All the recipes in this book serve four people unless stated otherwise. *Note:* 'A good pinch of either salt or sugar means roughly 25ml/½ tsp.

Menu suggestions appear at the beginning of each season. Do not regard them as absolute in any way: the book is divided into seasons because freshness is vital, but you are free to mix whatever dish you like with any others featured in the book. I'm sure you will also find that eating this way is bliss.

Notes

1 *Making Bread at Home*, Tom Jaine (Weidenfeld & Nicolson, London, 1995. This book, written by a master baker, tells you all you need to know about bread-making.
2 The best Indian vegetarian cookery books are those by Madhur Jaffrey and Julie Sahni.

WINTER

This season can seem rather dull with its emphasis on roots and pulses, but our system needs added carbohydrate at this time of year. Now, of course, there are many fresh green leaves imported from sunnier countries throughout the winter. Though I cannot feel one hundred per cent enthusiastic about imported foods in the supermarket, I have to admit that there are times when the palate needs diversity. Watercress, for example, now seems to be available throughout the winter months and is a wonderful source of iron and vitamins, good to eat raw. Spring onions are also in the shops throughout the year, making their name something of a misnomer. I find them a boon in salads and like them simply poached as a vegetable (see page 33). What makes winter special for me is all the grated salads I now make flavoured with rose, orange water and all manner of spices. These are so good that I urge you to start making them (see page 5). Delicious hot soups made from dried beans, lentils and peas also make winter a warm and pleasurable experience.

MENU SUGGESTIONS

Spicy Green Split Pea Soup, Potato Balls with Avocado and Corn Salsa, Sesame Brussels Sprouts, Fennel Salad, Prune and Coconut Cream.

—

Leek, Lime and Coconut Soup, Potato and Artichoke Stew, Winter Mixed Salad with Tahini Dressing, Apricot Tart.

—

Parsnip and Orange Soup, Mixed Aubergine Stew, Broccoli with Lime Shoyu, Cabbage, Mustard and Peanut Salad, fresh fruit or Caramelised Pineapple.

—

Garlic, Saffron and Almond Soup, Red Bean and Potato Chilli, Spinach and Avocado Salad, Dried Fruit Tart.

—

Spinach Soup with Garlic Croûtons, Baked Beans and Potatoes, Celeriac Chips, Red Cabbage and Apricot Salad, Pecan Pie.

—

Celeriac and Ginger Soup, Potato and Tempeh Gratin, Stir-fried Cabbage with Marmalade and Pine Nuts, Leaf Salad, Sussex Pond Pudding.

—

French Onion Soup, Green Peppers Stuffed with Avocado Purée, Sweet and Sour Red Cabbage, Carrot, Almond and Rose Salad, Spotted Dick.

—

Haricot Bean Soup and Gremolata, Baked Orange Vegetables, Curried Parsnip Purée, Beetroot and Mango Salad, Twelfth Night Cake.

—

1

❄ WINTER SOUPS ❄

❄ SPICY GREEN SPLIT PEA SOUP ❄

110g/4oz green split peas
30ml/2 tbsp olive oil
2 onions, peeled and chopped
2 garlic cloves, peeled and chopped
1 green chilli, deseeded and chopped

1.75 litres/3 pints water
1 vegetable stock cube
sea salt and freshly ground black pepper
handful green coriander, chopped

Pour boiling water over the dried split peas, covering them by about 2.5cm/1 inch. Leave for 30 minutes. Heat the oil in a large saucepan and throw in the onions, garlic and chilli. Sweat in the oil for a minute, then add the peas and their soaking water plus the rest of the water and the stock cube. Bring to the boil and simmer for 30 minutes. Leave to cool, season, then blend. Bring back to the boil slowly (you may need a little more water or stock) and add the chopped coriander before serving.

❄ LEEK, LIME AND COCONUT SOUP ❄

30ml/2 tbsp sesame oil
3 medium leeks, cleaned and thinly sliced
1 green chilli, seeded and chopped
2 medium potatoes, peeled and sliced

zest and juice of 2 limes
1.2 litres/2 pints water
1 vegetable stock cube
570ml/1 pint coconut milk
handful green coriander, chopped

Heat the sesame oil in a large saucepan and throw in the leeks, chilli and potatoes. Sweat for a moment before adding the water and stock cube. Bring to the boil, then simmer for 20 minutes. Season and add the coconut milk and lime juice. Add the chopped coriander before serving.

❄ PARSNIP AND ORANGE SOUP ❄

30ml/2 tbsp olive oil
2 medium parsnips, peeled and
chopped
5ml/1 tsp mustard seed
5ml/1 tsp cardamom seeds

1.2 litres/2 pints water
1 vegetable stock cube
zest and juice of 2 large oranges
sea salt and freshly ground black
pepper

Heat the oil in a pan and add the parsnips, mustard and cardamom seeds. Cook for a moment, stirring, until the seeds begin to pop, then add the water and the stock cube. Bring to the boil and simmer for 10 minutes, then add the orange zest and seasoning. Blend to a purée and add the orange juice. Reheat without boiling.

❄ GARLIC, SAFFRON AND ALMOND SOUP ❄

1 head of garlic (10 or 12 large
cloves)
45ml/3 tbsp olive oil
good pinch saffron
1.2 litres/2 pints water
570ml/1 pint soya milk

110g/4oz ground almonds
sea salt and freshly ground black
pepper
30–45ml/2–3 tbsp roasted almond
flakes, or handful of chopped
parsley

Pour boiling water over the garlic cloves, leave for 5 minutes, then peel them. Heat the olive oil, add the garlic and saffron and cook for a moment before adding the water. Bring to the boil and simmer for 15 minutes, then leave to cool. Blend the mixture, then pour back into a pan. Add the soya milk, almonds and seasoning and reheat. Roast the almond flakes (if using) in a dry saucepan until they turn golden brown, and sprinkle over the soup before serving. Alternatively, use a little chopped parsley.

❄ SPINACH SOUP WITH GARLIC CROÛTONS ❄

30ml/2 tbsp olive oil
450g/1lb spinach leaves, without stalks
1 large potato, diced
570ml/1 pint water
1 vegetable stock cube
570ml/1 pint soya milk

sea salt and freshly ground black pepper

Garlic croûtons
2 or 3 thick pieces stale brown bread
30–45ml/2 or 3 tbsp olive oil
2 or 3 garlic cloves, crushed

Heat the oil in a pan, add the spinach leaves and diced potato and cook for a moment. Then add the water and stock cube. Bring to the boil, then simmer for 15 minutes. Blend the mixture, add the soya milk and seasoning, then reheat gently.

To make the croûtons, cut the bread into small cubes about 5mm/¼ inch square. Heat the oil in a frying pan and throw in the garlic and diced bread. Stir-fry over a high heat until the cubes are golden brown. Serve in a separate bowl.

❄ CELERIAC AND GINGER SOUP ❄

45ml/3 tbsp olive oil
2 medium celeriac, peeled and chopped
55g/2oz ginger root, peeled and sliced very thinly

1.2 litres/2 pints water
1 vegetable stock cube
570ml/1 pint soya milk
sea salt and freshly ground black pepper

Heat the olive oil in a pan and throw in the celeriac and ginger; cook for a moment, then add the water and vegetable stock. Bring to the boil, then simmer for 15 minutes. Blend the mixture, add the soya milk and seasoning and reheat gently. Serve with garlic croûtons (see above).

❄ FRENCH ONION SOUP ❄

30ml/2 tbsp olive oil	1.2 litres/2 pints water
900g/2lb onions, peeled and sliced	3 vegetable stock cubes (reduced salt)
15ml/1 tbsp caster sugar	freshly ground black pepper

Heat the oil in a pan and throw in the onions and sugar. Cook over a medium heat for 15–20 minutes, or until the onions have caramelised: they should be golden tinged with darkish brown to black. Add the water and stock cubes, bring to the boil and simmer for 10 minutes. (The stock has to be strong, but do use reduced-salt stock cubes or the finished soup will be far too salty.) Serve the soup with slightly charred toast, ideally prepared over a charcoal grill.

❄ HARICOT BEAN SOUP AND GREMOLATA ❄

45ml/3 tbsp olive oil	freshly ground black pepper
110g/4oz haricot beans	
2 onions, peeled and sliced	*For the gremolata*
1 celeriac, peeled and sliced	45ml/3 tbsp finely chopped
1 celery heart, sliced	parsley
1.75 litres/3 pints water	4 garlic cloves, finely diced
2 vegetable stock cubes	zest of 3 lemons

Pour boiling water over the haricot beans and leave for 1 hour. Heat the oil in a large pan, throw in the onions, celeriac and celery, then add the drained beans. Cook for a moment or two, then add the water and stock cubes. Bring to the boil and simmer for about 1 hour.

Make the gremolata by mixing the parsley, garlic and lemon zest together. Place in a bowl and allow people to help themselves by sprinkling a little into their soup.

❄ WINTER SALADS ❄

❄ CARROT, ALMOND AND ROSE SALAD ❄

30ml/2 tbsp rose water
15ml/1 tbsp raspberry vinegar
45ml/3 tbsp olive oil
5ml/1 tsp sea salt
5ml/1 tsp caster sugar

4 large carrots, finely grated
2 tbsp roasted almonds, coarsely chopped
green ends of 4 spring onions, thinly sliced

In a large bowl mix together the rose water, vinegar, oil, salt and sugar, beating thoroughly. Add the grated carrots and toss so that everything is coated in the dressing. Stir in the chopped almonds and toss again. Leave for 1 hour before serving, then stir in the sliced spring onions.

Here are two slightly different salads both using cabbage and peanuts. These ingredients are a favourite combination of mine.

❄ SAVOY CABBAGE, MUSTARD AND PEANUT SALAD ❄

2 garlic cloves, crushed
30ml/2 tbsp white wine vinegar
60ml/4 tbsp olive oil
15ml/1 tbsp wholegrain mustard

1 medium Savoy cabbage, finely grated
30ml/2 tbsp salted peanuts, crushed

In a large bowl mix the crushed garlic with the vinegar, olive oil and mustard. Add the cabbage and toss well. Sprinkle the crushed peanuts over the salad and toss again. Leave for 1 hour before serving.

❋ Red Cabbage and Peanut Salad ❋

90ml/6 tbsp olive oil

10ml/2 tsp mustard seeds

2 garlic cloves, crushed

10ml/2 tsp cardamom pods, seeds extracted

15ml/1 tbsp red wine vinegar

15ml/1 tbsp orange water

zest of 1 orange

2 green chillies, seeded and finely diced

5ml/1 tsp sea salt

2.5ml/½ tsp caster sugar

1 medium red cabbage, grated

45ml/3 tbsp salted peanuts, finely crushed

Heat 30ml/2 tbsp olive oil and sauté the mustard seeds, chillies, garlic and cardamom seeds until the mustard begins to pop. Place the mixture in a large salad bowl. Add the vinegar, orange water, orange zest, salt, sugar and the remaining olive oil and combine thoroughly. Add the grated cabbage to the salad bowl and toss so that it is covered with the dressing. Finally, add the salted peanuts to the salad, toss thoroughly and serve.

❋ Fennel Salad ❋

2 or 3 heads of fennel

juice of 1 lemon

5ml/1 tsp sea salt

Cut the feathery tops off the fennel and reserve. Discard the tough outside leaves and stalks, then slice the bulbs vertically from top to bottom in five or six pieces. Lay them on a large platter. Chop the feathery leaves and sprinkle over the fennel, followed by the lemon juice and sea salt. Serve at once. Eat with the fingers.

❋ WINTER MIXED SALAD WITH TAHINI DRESSING ❋

110g/4oz mixed sprouting seeds
450g/1lb cherry tomatoes, cut in half
bunch of spring onions, thinly sliced
1 heart of celery, cut into 1cm/½ inch
pieces
2 Little Gem lettuces, cut into 1cm/½
inch pieces

For the tahini dressing
45ml/3 tbsp water
45ml/3 tbsp olive oil
45ml/3 tbsp juice and zest of 1
lemon
1 garlic clove, crushed
30ml/2 tbsp smooth, light tahini

Place the sprouting seeds in a large bowl, then add the tomatoes, spring onions, celery and lettuce.

To make the dressing, place all the ingredients in a blender and mix to a smooth purée about the consistency of thin cream; if too thick, add a little more water. Pour over the salad and toss thoroughly.

❋ SPINACH AND AVOCADO SALAD ❋

3 or 4 leaves of sage, chopped
10ml/2 tsp white wine vinegar
60ml/4 tbsp olive oil
10ml/2 tsp green peppercorns in
brine, drained
pinch of sea salt and freshly

ground black pepper
1 ripe avocado, peeled and sliced
225g/8oz young spinach leaves,
washed and dried
handful of garlic croûtons (see
page 4)

Place the sage, vinegar, olive oil, peppercorns and seasoning in a large bowl. Add the avocado strips to the dressing and toss gently. Then add the spinach leaves and toss again. Finally, sprinkle with the croûtons and serve.

❄ RED CABBAGE AND APRICOT SALAD ❄

6 dried apricots

30ml/2 tbsp sultanas

1 glass dry sherry

30ml/2 tbsp orange flower water

15ml/1 tbsp raspberry vinegar

75ml/5 tbsp olive oil

sea salt and freshly ground black

pepper to taste

1 small red cabbage, finely grated

Soak the apricots and sultanas in the sherry overnight. Make the dressing in a large bowl by mixing together the orange flower water, vinegar, olive oil and seasoning. Beat well then add the grated cabbage and dried fruits. Toss thoroughly and leave for 1 hour before serving.

❄ BEETROOT AND MANGO SALAD ❄

1 red chilli, deseeded and sliced

paper thin

15ml/1 tbsp red wine vinegar

5ml/1 tsp Dijon mustard

60ml/4 tbsp olive oil

sea salt and freshly ground black

pepper

4 or 5 medium, uncooked

beetroots, peeled and grated

110g/4oz sliced dried mango,

finely diced

1 red onion, thinly sliced

In a large bowl mix together the chilli, vinegar, mustard, oil and seasoning. Add the beetroots and mango and toss well. Sprinkle the sliced red onion on top and serve.

❋ CHINESE CABBAGE AND SATAY SALAD ❋

450g/1lb Chinese cabbage, inner leaves only, chopped across into 1cm/½ inch pieces
bunch of spring onions, thinly sliced
1 green chilli, deseeded and thinly sliced

15ml/1 tbsp rice wine vinegar
1 garlic clove, crushed
30ml/2 tbsp sesame oil
30ml/2 tbsp smooth peanut butter
juice and zest of 1 lemon
sea salt and freshly ground black pepper

Blanch the Chinese cabbage for 2 minutes. Drain thoroughly by using a salad spinner. Make the dressing in a large bowl by mixing together the chilli, vinegar, garlic, oil, peanut butter, lemon juice and zest with some seasoning. The mixture should be smooth and creamy: if too thick, add a little water or oil. Toss the cabbage and the onion in the dressing and serve garnished with a little more green onion.

❄ WINTER MAIN DISHES ❄

In the winter vegetable stews are warm and comforting, but in my book they must also be tasty and stimulating. I enjoy the heat of chillies, so I always use the whole pod, but in the following recipes I have specified just the skin. It's your choice.

To thicken sauces at the end of cooking, simply remove some of the potatoes, beans and liquid from the pan, blend them and pour back into the stew.

Many of the recipes include beans, but there is no need to soak them overnight: if you do so, they can sometimes start to ferment. Simply pour boiling water over the beans and leave for 1 hour before using.

❄ POTATO, CARROT AND ARTICHOKE STEW ❄

45ml/3 tbsp olive oil
3 or 4 garlic cloves
2 onions, sliced
2 celery hearts, sliced
450g/1lb baby potatoes
200g/7oz carrots, diced

1.2 litres/2 pints vegetable stock
225g/8oz tin artichoke bottoms, drained
sea salt and freshly ground black pepper
large handful parsley, chopped

Heat the olive oil in a large saucepan and throw in the garlic, onions, celery, carrots and potatoes. Stir and cook for a moment or two before adding the vegetable stock. Bring to the boil and simmer for 20 minutes, then add the artichokes and seasoning. Return to the heat and just before serving stir in the chopped parsley. Serve with rice, bulgar wheat or fettucini and a mixed salad of leaves.

❄ BEAN AND MUSHROOM STEW ❄

45ml/3 tbsp olive oil

3 garlic cloves, crushed

1 green chilli, deseeded

225g/8oz cultivated mushrooms, sliced

2 onions, sliced

110g/4oz haricot beans, soaked for 1 hour

110g/4oz flageolet beans, soaked for 1 hour

110g/4oz dried porcini, soaked for 1 hour

1.2 litres/2 pints vegetable stock

30ml/2 tbsp soy sauce

sea salt and freshly ground black pepper

handful coriander, chopped

Heat the olive oil in a pan and throw in the garlic, chilli, mushrooms and onions. Cook for a few minutes, stirring so that they do not stick. Add both types of beans and the porcini with their soaking water and the vegetable stock. Bring to the boil and simmer for 1 hour. Check the pan halfway through to see if the beans need any more liquid: add another 290ml/½ pint if they do. If you want the sauce to be thicker, take some of the beans out of the stew and blend them to a mush, then stir them back in. Add the soy sauce and seasoning, then taste and adjust if necessary. Stir in the coriander and serve with noodles and a green salad.

❄ BAKED ORANGE VEGETABLES ❄

4 smallish parsnips, peeled and halved

4 small kohlrabi, peeled and halved

4 medium onions, peeled

4 smallish potatoes, peeled and halved

5ml/1 tsp sea salt

zest and juice of 2 oranges

1 green chilli, deseeded and finely chopped

30ml/2 tbsp maple syrup

30ml/2 tbsp olive oil

30ml/2 tbsp thick-cut marmalade

Boil the parsnips, kohlrabi, onions and potatoes for about 3 minutes. Mix together the salt, orange juice and zest, chilli, maple syrup and oil to make a cooking marinade. Drain the boiled vegetables carefully, tip them into a baking tray and pour the marinade over them. Place in a hot oven 200°C/400°F/Gas mark 6 for 45 minutes. Halfway through the cooking time, turn the vegetables and baste them. When ready, they should be browned and slightly caramelised. Pour off the cooking juices and mix with the marmalade. Place the vegetables on a platter, pour the sauce over them and serve.

✳ POTATO BALLS WITH AVOCADO AND CORN SALSA ✳

4 large old potatoes, peeled and chopped
60ml/4 tbsp olive oil
1 green chilli, deseeded
2 garlic cloves, crushed
bunch of spring onions, thinly sliced
sea salt and freshly ground black pepper
30–45ml/2–3 tbsps sesame seeds
sunflower oil for frying

For the Avocado and Corn Salsa*
225g/8oz frozen corn, thawed and drained, or 2 fresh cobs,

boiled, cooled and dehusked
3 ripe avocados, peeled, stoned and cubed
2 red onions, thinly sliced
1 small red pepper, finely diced
3 garlic cloves, finely chopped
120ml/4 fl oz olive oil
30ml/1 fl oz red wine vinegar
15ml/1 tbsp ground cumin
5 ml/1 tsp chilli powder
zest and juice of 3 limes
5ml/1 tsp Tabasco
5ml/1 tsp sea salt and freshly ground black pepper

* Adapted from *Salsas, Sambals, Chutneys and Chowchows* by Chris Schlesinger and John Willoughby (William Morrow and Co., New York, 1994).

Boil the potatoes in salted water for 15–20 minutes, or until cooked through. While they are cooking, heat the olive oil in a pan and cook the chilli, garlic and spring onions until the onions are softened. Reserve. When the potatoes are cooked, drain well and mash them. Add the onion and oil mixture and stir thoroughly. Flour your hands and roll the potato into golf-ball-sized pieces. Place the balls on greaseproof paper and refrigerate for 30 minutes. Roll each ball in the sesame seeds, then fry in the sunflower oil over a high heat until the outside is crisp and brown.

Mix all the salsa ingredients thoroughly, then cover and leave for 30 minutes before using.

❄ RED BEAN AND POTATO CHILLI ❄

45ml/3 tbsp olive oil
2 red chillies, sliced
3 garlic cloves, crushed
2 onions, sliced
110g/4oz red haricot beans, soaked for 1 hour
3 large potatoes, peeled and cut into chunks

6 small raw beetroot, peeled and halved
225g/8oz tin chopped tomatoes
half bottle red wine
1.2 litres/2 pints strong vegetable stock
sea salt and freshly ground black pepper

Heat the oil in a large pan and cook the chillies, garlic and onions for a few moments. Add the rest of the ingredients, except the salt, bring to the boil and simmer for 1 hour. When the beans and beetroot are tender, taste and adjust seasoning. Serve with gremolata (see page 5) to sprinkle over.

❄ MIXED AUBERGINE STEW ❄

45ml/3 tbsp olive oil
3 garlic cloves, chopped
1 red chilli, skinned, seeded and sliced
5ml/1 tsp mustard seeds
5ml/1 tsp coriander seeds, crushed
5ml/1 tsp ground cumin
2 onions, chopped
2 aubergines, trimmed and diced
3 courgettes, sliced into chunks
3 large potatoes, peeled and cut

into chunks
225g/8oz cultivated mushrooms, sliced
400g/14oz tin chopped tomatoes
1.2 litres/2 pints strong vegetable stock
225g/8oz tin chickpeas, drained
sea salt and freshly ground black pepper
handful fresh coriander leaves

Heat the oil in a large saucepan and throw in the garlic, chilli, spices and onions. Cook for a moment, stirring, to release the oils in the spices, then add all the vegetables with the tomatoes and stock. Bring to the boil, stirring, then simmer for 30 minutes. Stir in the drained chickpeas and add seasoning. Before serving, sprinkle with the fresh coriander.

❊ Baked Beans and Potatoes ❊

60ml/4 tbsp olive oil

1 red chilli, chopped

4 garlic cloves, chopped

2 onions, sliced

4 large potatoes, peeled and cut into chunks

170g/6oz navy (small haricot) beans soaked for 1 hour

2 × 400g/14oz tins chopped tomatoes

30ml/2 tbsp muscovado sugar

1.2 litres/2 pints vegetable stock

30ml/2 tbsp tomato purée

30ml/2 tbsp Dijon mustard

sea salt and freshly ground black pepper

Preheat the oven to 180°C/350°F/Gas mark 4. Heat the oil in a large casserole dish and throw in the chilli, garlic and onions. Cook until the onion is soft, then add the potatoes, the beans with their water, the chopped tomatoes, sugar and vegetable stock. Bring to the boil and place in the oven to cook for 3 hours. Once the beans are tender, add the tomato purée, mustard and seasoning.

❊ Potato and Tempeh Gratin ❊

2 large potatoes, peeled

60ml/4 tbsp olive oil

5ml/1 tsp cumin seeds

5ml/1 tsp mustard seeds

5ml/1 tsp coriander seeds, crushed

2 large onions, sliced

225g/8oz tempeh, defrosted and cut into 2.5cm/1 inch cubes

sea salt and freshly ground black pepper

handful green coriander, chopped

Par-boil the potatoes for 12–15 minutes, then drain and slice them into 5mm/¼ inch discs. Heat the oil in a large frying pan, add the spices and fry for a moment before adding the potatoes and onion. Fry for 2 minutes until beginning to brown, then add the tempeh. Continue to fry so that the potatoes brown and the tempeh gets a little crisp, about 2 minutes. Season, transfer to a platter and sprinkle the coriander over.

❆ WINTER SIDE DISHES ❆

A meal can be made up, as in the oriental manner, of many small dishes. In fact, if entertaining, this is the nicest way of giving a dinner party. Not all the dishes need be hot. We British make a fuss about the temperatures of food, but the flavours of a dish are often better revealed when the dish is warm and each mouthful can be savoured. Many of the following dishes can be prepared in advance and served cold or at room temperature; some can be prepared at the last moment. On the whole, a dish should never be warmed up, as it so easily tastes and looks disgusting. Some of these recipes, particularly the first three, make good starters.

❆ STUFFED NORI MOULDS ❆

zest and juice of 1 lemon

60ml/4 tbsp olive oil

5ml/1 tsp caraway seeds

sea salt and freshly ground black pepper

15ml/1 tbsp Dijon mustard

50ml/2 tbsp Plamil egg-free mayonnaise

2 ripe avocados

450g/1 lb small new potatoes, unpeeled, boiled and diced

bunch of spring onions, thinly cut

30ml/2 tbsp shoyu or soy sauce

1 packet nori sheets

bunch rocket leaves

few red geranium petals, for garnish

Mix the lemon juice and zest, olive oil, caraway and seasoning in a large bowl. Beat in the mustard and mayonnaise until you have a smooth, thickish dressing. Peel and stone the avocados, then dice the flesh into the dressing. Add the diced potatoes and spring onions. Toss gently but thoroughly.

Pour the shoyu into a shallow bowl (a soup bowl is ideal) and stir in the same amount of cold water. Place one of the dry nori sheets gently in the bowl so that it soaks up the mixture and becomes soft and pliable. Take an individual ramekin and lay the wet nori sheet inside it, gently pushing into the corners and allowing to overlap the sides. Spoon in enough potato and avocado mixture to reach the rim, then cover the top with the overhanging nori and smooth down. Refrigerate for 1 hour or a day. Before serving, unmould on to individual plates with a few rocket leaves at the side, sprinkle the shiny black surface with a few geranium petals and serve.

❊ POTATOES IN COCONUT CREAM ❊

900g/2lb potatoes, peeled and
sliced
30ml/2 tbsp olive oil
1 garlic clove, crushed
1 red or green chilli, seeded and
chopped
2 or 3 onions, thinly sliced
150ml/5 fl oz coconut cream
good pinch of sea salt
chopped coriander, for garnish

Boil the potatoes until just tender, then drain thoroughly. Heat the olive oil in a saucepan and add the garlic, chilli and onions. Lower the heat, cover the pan and leave to sweat for a few minutes. Now add the potatoes, turning them in the mixture, then add the coconut cream and salt. Continue to turn and let the potatoes reheat gently. Transfer to a serving dish and sprinkle with chopped coriander.

❊ SWEET AND SOUR SHALLOTS ❊

30ml/2 tbsp olive oil
450g/1lb shallots, peeled and
trimmed
45ml/3 tbsp red wine vinegar
15ml/1 tbsp muscovado sugar
sea salt and freshly ground black
pepper
few green spring onion tops,
chopped

Heat the oil in a large pan and throw in the whole shallots. Sauté for about 2 minutes, making sure they do not stick. Add the vinegar, sugar and seasoning, then cover the pan and cook for another 3 minutes. Pour into a dish and sprinkle with the chopped spring onions. This is good served right away, but may be eaten warm or cool.

❊ TURNIPS WITH GINGER ❊

450g/1lb small purple turnips, trimmed
45ml/3 tbsp olive oil
55g/2oz root ginger, peeled and finely diced
3 garlic cloves, crushed
1 green chilli, thinly sliced, pith and seeds removed
sea salt and freshly ground black pepper
juice and zest of 1 lemon

Cut the turnips in half and throw them into a pan of boiling salted water for 1 minute. Drain. Heat the oil in a frying pan and add the ginger, garlic and chilli. Fry for a few moments before adding the turnips. Fry for 3–4 minutes, turning so that they brown evenly. Remove the pan from the heat and add the seasoning, lemon juice and zest. Tip into a dish and serve.

❊ CURRIED PARSNIP PURÉE ❊

675g/1½lb parsnips, peeled
45ml/3 tbsp olive oil
10ml/2 tsp ground fenugreek
15ml/1 tbsp garam masala
5ml/1 tsp cumin seeds
5ml/1 tsp mustard seeds
sea salt and freshly ground black pepper

Cut the parsnips into chunks and boil in salted water for 4 minutes or until tender. Drain well and mash thoroughly. Heat the olive oil, throw in the cumin and mustard seeds and cook for a moment to release the oils. Remove from the heat and add the fenugreek. Pour this mixture into the mashed parsnips. Add the garam masala and seasoning. Beat the mixture until smooth, adding a little more oil if necessary.

❈ STIR-FRIED CABBAGE WITH MARMALADE AND PINE NUTS ❈

15ml/1 tbsp sesame oil
1 medium Savoy cabbage, thinly sliced
30ml/2 tbsp pine nuts
sea salt and freshly ground black pepper
30ml/2 tbsp thick-cut marmalade

Heat the oil in a wok or frying pan and throw in the cabbage. Stir-fry for 2 minutes, then add the pine nuts and seasoning. Fry for another minute, then add the marmalade. Toss thoroughly and serve.

❈ BROCCOLI WITH LIME SHOYU ❈

450g/1lb broccoli, broken into small florets
30ml/2 tbsp olive oil
1 green chilli, thinly sliced, skin and pith removed
zest and juice of 2 limes
45ml/3 tbsp shoyu or soy sauce

Throw the broccoli into boiling salted water and simmer for 2 minutes. Drain and set aside. Heat the oil in a pan and fry the chilli for a few moments before adding the broccoli, lime zest and juice and the shoyu or soy sauce. Stir for 1 minute, then transfer to a serving dish.

❆ Sweet and Sour Red Cabbage ❆

45ml/3 tbsp sunflower oil
5 garlic cloves, finely chopped
and thinly sliced
45ml/3 tbsp red wine vinegar
30ml/2 tbsp muscovado sugar

2 dried red chillies, broken up
1 medium red cabbage, trimmed
sea salt and freshly ground black
pepper

Heat the oil in a large casserole dish and fry the garlic and chillies for a few moments. Add the cabbage and remaining ingredients. Bring to the boil, then place in a preheated oven at 180°C/350°F/Gas mark 4 and leave for 3 hours. Alternatively, cook on the hob over a low heat for about the same amount of time. The cabbage should have reduced to a third of its bulk and be slightly caramelised. Taste and adjust seasoning.

❆ Sesame Brussels Sprouts ❆

450g/1lb small Brussels sprouts,
trimmed
30ml/2 tbsp sesame seeds, roasted

30ml/2 tbsp toasted sesame oil
sea salt and freshly ground black
pepper

Grate the Brussels sprouts (easy in a food processor). Roast the sesame seeds by putting them into a dry saucepan over a high heat and shaking the pan until they have turned golden brown. Reserve. In another pan heat the sesame oil and throw in the grated sprouts. Stir over the heat until they have wilted to about half their bulk. Finally, sprinkle in the seeds, season and serve. This dish is also excellent served cold as a salad.

❆ Celeriac Chips ❆

2 small celeriac, peeled and
trimmed
45ml/3 tbsp olive oil

zest and juice of 1 lemon
sea salt and freshly ground black
pepper

Slice the celeriac into 5mm/¼ inch rounds, then cut these into chip size. Heat the olive oil and fry the chips until brown. Before serving, sprinkle with the lemon zest and juice and seasoning.

❆ WINTER PUDDINGS ❆

Winter is the season when we need more carbohydrates to keep warm, so we can indulge ourselves in a few steamed puddings. There is no doubt in my mind that vegetarian suet, which can be easily purchased now, gives a far lighter pastry and a better flavour than traditional shredded beef suet. Do not kid yourself, however, that vegetarian suet is a healthy option: it is just as high in saturated fats as beef suet because it is made from palm oil, which is then hydrogenated. An alternative to vegetable suet is ground brazil nuts used in the same proportion of fat to flour. Brazil nuts will give you a lighter, almost sponge-like suet with a pleasant, nutty flavour.

❆ SUSSEX POND PUDDING ❆

fat for greasing a 1.2 litre/2 pint pudding basin

5m/1 tsp caster sugar
a little water

For the pastry
340g/12oz self-raising flour
170g/6oz vegetarian suet or ground brazil nuts
pinch of salt

For the filling
2 lemons, cut into quarters
60ml/4 tbsp muscovado sugar
90ml/6 tbsp soya cream

Put all the pastry ingredients, except for the water, into a mixing bowl and stir thoroughly. Add the water slowly, just enough to make the flour and fat come together into a soft dough. Pummel it a little so that it is pliable. Set aside one third of the pastry and roll out the remainder on a floured surface until large enough to line the pudding basin. Arrange the lemon wedges in the lined basin, cover with the sugar and pour in the cream. Roll out the reserved pastry and use to cover the basin, pressing the edges together to seal them. Cover with foil and a cloth, tie with string and lower into a saucepan of boiling water slightly lower than the string. Place the pan on a low flame and simmer for 2–3 hours. Remove the basin and leave to rest for 10 minutes. Unwrap the pudding, cover with a plate and gently upturn it. Take care when you cut into it as the contents will spill out.

❋ SPOTTED DICK ❋

60ml/4 tbsp currants
60ml/4 tbsp sultanas
55g/2oz dried apricots
55g/2oz dried pineapple
55g/2oz crystallised ginger
sweet sherry, Madeira or Marsala
fat for greasing 1.2 litre/2 pint
pudding basin

For the dough
350g/12oz self-raising flour
170g/6oz vegetarian suet or
ground brazil nuts
pinch of salt
15ml/1 tbsp caster sugar

The night before needed, marinate all the dried fruits in sweet sherry, Madeira or Marsala. To make the dough, mix together the flour, fat and salt. Add the fruit and liquid and form a dough; if sloppy, add more flour. Roll into a ball and place in the greased pudding basin. Cover and steam as Sussex Pond Pudding. Serve with a jam sauce poured over it.

❋ APRICOT TART ❋

For the pastry
170g/6oz plain flour
55g/2oz soya flour
15ml/1 tbsp caster sugar
5ml/1 tsp salt
110g/4oz vegetable fat, frozen then grated
45ml/3 tbsp soya cream

For the filling
225g/8oz dried apricots, soaked overnight
225g/8oz soya cream
45ml/3 tbsp brandy
45ml/3 tbsp muscovado sugar

Make the pastry by mixing together the flours, sugar and salt and rubbing in the grated vegetable fat. Add the cream to bind the mixture. Mould into a ball and refrigerate for 30 minutes. Return to room temperature before rolling out and use to line a 20cm/8 inch tart tin.

Place the apricots and their soaking water in a saucepan over a gentle heat and cook until tender and all the water has evaporated, about 3 minutes. Blend half the apricots to a purée, add the soya cream and brandy and pour the mixture into the pastry shell. Place the rest of the apricots in a pattern on top of the purée. Then bend the sides over onto the apricots and mark with a knife to make a scallop shell effect. Sprinkle the sugar over the top and bake in a preheated oven at 220°C/425°F/Gas mark 7 for 15–20 minutes. Leave to cool before slicing.

❄ TWELFTH NIGHT CAKE ❄

I have adapted this recipe from one which appears in Marie Pierre Moine's delightful book *The Festive Food of France*.

300g/10½oz puff pastry
a little soya milk for glazing

For the filling
170g/6oz ground almonds
zest of 2 oranges

45ml/3 tbsp orange marmalade
15ml/1 tbsp kirsch or orange liqueur
100g/3½oz vegetable fat, softened
100g/3½oz caster sugar

Preheat the oven to 200°C/400°F/Gas mark 6. Divide the puff pastry in half and roll the two pieces into circles about 20–25cm/8–10 inches wide. Grease a baking sheet and place one circle into the centre. Combine all the filling ingredients and spread over the pastry circle, leaving a 2.5cm/1 inch border all round. Use a pastry brush to paint this border with the soya milk. Carefully place the second pastry circle over the filling and gently press around the edges to seal it. Prick the pastry with a fork and make a lattice-work pattern on top with a sharp knife. Brush the surface with soya milk, then bake in the oven for 20–30 minutes, or until the whole cake is puffed up and brown. Serve warm.

❄ PRUNE AND COCONUT CREAM ❄

225g/8oz prunes
225g/8oz tin coconut cream
30ml/2 tbsp brandy

30ml/2 tbsp caster sugar
2 tbsp grated dark chocolate

* Very black chocolate has no milk solids added to it, so it is the true taste of chocolate. Although expensive, a little used as flavouring, as in this recipe, is heavenly.

Soak the prunes overnight, then take the stones out. Cook them briefly in their soaking water until quite tender and the water has evaporated, about 4 minutes. Blend them with the coconut cream, brandy and sugar, then pour into 4 individual glasses and refrigerate for a few hours. Sprinkle the chocolate over and serve.

❄ DRIED FRUIT TART ❄

1 pastry case, baked blind
55g/2oz dried apple rings
55g/2oz dried pears
55g/2oz dried pineapple
55g/2oz dried apricots
55g/2oz currants
55g/2oz sultanas

55g/2oz crystallised ginger
30ml/2 tbsp rose water
30ml/2 tbsp dark rum
zest of 1 orange and 1 lemon
30ml/2 tbsp dark muscovado
sugar

To bake blind: place pastry case in a hot oven for five minutes. Fill with ceramic beans so that the centre does not puff up.

Put all the dried fruits into a mixing bowl, cover them with boiling water and leave overnight. Tip the lot into a saucepan and heat gently for 5 minutes until the fruit is tender and all the water has evaporated. Add the rose water, rum and orange and lemon zest. Stir thoroughly, then pour into the pastry case, pressing down gently and arranging the fruit attractively. Now arrange the crystallised ginger on top in any pattern that appeals to you. Sprinkle with sugar and bake in a hot oven at 220°C/425°F/Gas mark 7 for 20 minutes. Leave to cool before slicing.

❄ PECAN PIE ❄

1 pastry case, baked blind (see
Dried Fruit Tart, page 19)
30ml/2 tbsp arrowroot powder
225g/8oz muscovado sugar
75g/3oz vegetable fat
2.5ml/½ tsp salt

5ml/1 tsp vanilla essence
90ml/6 tbsp golden syrup
225g/8oz shelled pecan nuts,
coarsely chopped, plus a few
whole ones for decoration

Preheat the oven to 200°C/400°F/Gas mark 6. Mix the arrowroot with the sugar then add the fat and mix to a cream. Add the salt and vanilla essence, then stir in the golden syrup. Add the chopped pecan nuts, then pour the mixture into the pastry case and decorate with the whole nuts. Bake for 30 minutes. Leave to cool before slicing.

❄ CARAMELISED PINEAPPLE ❄

1 whole ripe pineapple
sunflower oil
45ml/3 tbsp caster sugar

100ml/3½ fl oz dark rum for
deglazing

First prepare the pineapple. Cut the top and bottom off, then peel off the outside with a sharp knife. Slice in half lengthways, then cut out the core from both halves. Slice each half lengthways into six equal pieces. Heat a little oil in a large frying pan, add 2 or 3 pieces of pineapple, sprinkle with sugar and fry, turning the pieces until they are brown and beginning to caramelise. Cook all the pineapple in this way, adding more oil as you need it. Arrange the pineapple on individual plates. Deglaze the pan by pouring the rum into it, turning up the heat and scraping the bottom until the sauce bubbles. Pour a little of the sauce over each piece of pineapple and serve.

SPRING

T his is the season which stimulates the salivary glands, the thought of all those new green shoots thrusting through the frosty earth, burgeoning with taste and growth. So much is growing – the first sorrel leaves to make a wonderful soup or just to have as a sauce, the first baby spinach leaves and the new leaves of rocket, plump little beetroots and delicate young rhubarb, much maligned ingredients which have only recently come into their own. Then later there are the first baby broad beans, peas and mange-tout, and the first thinnings from lettuce, endive and chicory. It is the season when we need do little to such vegetables, but steam them and eat them with good olive oil and a little sea salt.

MENU SUGGESTIONS

Iced Avocado
Soup,
Mushroom
Risotto, Fresh
Peas with
Shredded
Lettuce, Leek,
Almond and
Caper Salad,
Rhubarb Sorbet.

—

Iced Spicy
Avocado Soup,
Potato and
Onion Gratin,
Radicchio and
Red Bean Salad,
Warm Walnut
and Spinach
Salad, Simple
Grape Pudding.

—

Gazpacho,
Spinach Risotto,
Poached Spring
Onions, Leaf
Salad, Apricot
Cream.

—

Fresh Green Pea
Soup, Wild Rice
Pilaf, Celery,
Carrot and
Tahini Salad,
Mango Coconut
Cream.

—

Pasta with
Spring Sauce,
Broad Bean and
Green Pepper
and Courgette
Soup,

Walnut Salad,
Leaf Salad,
Rum, Coconut
and Date
Cream.

—

Chilled Lettuce
and Melon
Soup, Linguine
con Piselli,
Broad Beans
with Tomato,
Oregano and
Basil Sauce,
Cherry Fool.

—

Bortsch, Spicy
Green
Indonesian
Vegetable Stew,

Aubergine and
Courgette
Slices, Prune
Tartlets with
Rum Sauce.

—

Chinese
Cabbage Soup,
Indonesian Rice
Noodles,
Grated
Courgettes with
Walnuts,
Spinach,
Avocado and
Peanut Salad,
Rhubarb and
Ginger
Roulade.

❧ SPRING SOUPS ❧

❧ ICED AVOCADO SOUP ❧

3 ripe avocados

290ml/10 fl oz strong vegetable stock

sea salt and freshly ground black

pepper

45ml/3 tbsp chopped green coriander

leaf coriander for garnish

Blend the avocado flesh with the other ingredients until fairly thick and creamy-smooth. Pour into a large tureen or bowl, cover and refrigerate for 1 hour. Sprinkle the leaf coriander over the surface before serving.

❧ ICED SPICY AVOCADO SOUP ❧

30ml/2 tbsp olive oil

1 green chilli, finely chopped

2 garlic cloves, crushed

3 ripe avocados, peeled and

stoned

570ml/1 pint soya milk

sea salt and freshly ground black pepper

Heat the olive oil in a pan and throw in the chilli and garlic. Cook for a moment so that the oil is flavoured. Then add this mixture to the ripe avocado flesh which has been blended with the milk and seasoning, and refrigerate as in the previous recipe. This gives a thinner soup but with an excellent flavour.

❧ Gazpacho ❧

450g/lb tomatoes, skinned
1 garlic clove, crushed
1 cucumber, chopped
1 green pepper, seeded and chopped
1 red pepper, seeded and chopped
1 green chilli, chopped

30ml/2 tbsp olive oil
juice and zest of 1 lemon
sea salt and freshly ground black pepper
175ml/6 fl oz strong vegetable stock
green leaf coriander for garnish

Place the first nine ingredients in a blender and blend briefly; do not reduce to a complete pulp or there will be no texture in the soup. Add the stock, then taste and adjust the seasoning if necessary. Refrigerate for 1 hour or so, then serve with ice cubes and a little chopped coriander.

❧ Fresh Green Pea Soup ❧

700g/1lb 9oz fresh peas
1.2 litres/2 pints vegetable stock
sea salt and freshly ground black

pepper
chopped mint, for garnish
soya cream (optional)

Pod the peas and cook the pods in 570ml/1 pint of the stock until they are soft. Leave to cool, then blend the pods with their liquor. Strain through a sieve and reserve. Now cook the peas in the remaining stock; when just cooked, blend these too. Mix the two liquids together and reheat gently. Season to taste and before serving scatter the chopped mint over the surface. A spoonful of soya cream can also be added before serving, if you wish.

Variation: Use young broad beans and their pods instead of peas.

❧ CHINESE CABBAGE SOUP ❧

30ml/2 tbsp sesame oil

55g/2oz ginger root, peeled and thinly sliced

3 or 4 garlic cloves, thinly sliced

1 green chilli, finely chopped

1 Chinese cabbage, finely chopped

10ml/2 tsp tamarind paste

zest and juice of 2 limes

glass of dry sherry

290ml/10 fl oz strong vegetable stock

sea salt and freshly ground black pepper

Heat the sesame oil and sweat the ginger, garlic and chilli for a few moments, then add the chopped cabbage. Cook over a low heat for 3 minutes, then add the tamarind paste, the lime zest and juice, the sherry and stock. Stir and leave for a few minutes. Check the seasoning before serving.

❧ CHILLED LETTUCE AND MELON SOUP ❧

45ml/3 tbsp olive oil

1 large cos lettuce, chopped

5 or 6 shallots, sliced

1 garlic clove, crushed

5ml/1 tsp dried green peppercorns

bunch of watercress

500ml/18 fl oz vegetable stock

sea salt and freshly ground black pepper

50ml/1 tsp caster sugar

1 medium Ogen or Charentais melon

Heat the olive oil in a saucepan and throw in the lettuce, shallots, garlic, peppercorns and watercress. Place a lid on the pan and leave the contents to sweat over a low heat for a few minutes. When the vegetables are softened, add the stock, seasoning and sugar. Simmer for a few moments more. Meanwhile, deseed the melon, place the flesh in a blender and reduce to a thin purée. Set aside. Blend the lettuce and watercress to a purée, then combine with the melon purée. Refrigerate for 1 hour before serving.

🌿 BORTSCH 🌿

30ml/2 tbsp olive oil

5 or 6 small raw beetroots, peeled and chopped

1 garlic clove, crushed

juice and zest of 2 oranges

860ml/1½ pints vegetable stock

1 large glass dry sherry

sea salt and freshly ground black pepper

Heat the oil in a pan and throw in the garlic beetroots and orange zest. Pour in the vegetable stock and simmer for hour. Leave to cool, then blend to a purée. Add the orange juice, sherry and seasoning. Refrigerate for 1 hour or reheat gently.

Note: Bortsch is one of those soups that has as many interpretations as *Hamlet*. I have made complicated recipes with a dozen different vegetables and also the very simple one above. They are all delicious, but do ensure you use only tender young beetroot.

🌿 GREEN PEPPER AND COURGETTE SOUP 🌿

30ml/2 tbsp olive oil

2 garlic cloves, crushed

1 green chilli, seeded and chopped

5 green peppers, seeded and chopped

5 medium courgettes, trimmed and chopped

860ml/1½ pints vegetable stock

sea salt and freshly ground black pepper

Heat the oil in a saucepan and throw in the garlic, chilli, peppers and courgettes. Place a lid on the pan and let the vegetables cook slowly over a low heat until soft. Add the stock and seasoning, simmer for a moment more, then blend and reheat gently.

❧ SPRING SALADS ❧

We think of salads mostly as consisting of various lettuce leaves. Such concoctions are refreshing to eat after a main course, but salads can be made of almost every vegetable and fruit, especially in spring when all the young vegetables are being harvested. So be adventurous and do not be afraid of contriving warm salads, where the vegetables have been briefly cooked and are just singed or wilted. They give you the benefits of both raw and slightly caramelised flavours plus texture – an excellent combination.

❧ LEEK, ALMOND AND CAPER SALAD ❧

2 or 3 medium leeks, trimmed

3 or 4 spring onions, trimmed

45ml/3 tbsp olive oil

55g/2oz flaked almonds

10ml/2 tsp red wine vinegar

15ml/1 tbsp maple syrup

5ml/1 tsp garam masala

zest and juice of 1 lime

sea salt and freshly ground black pepper

15ml/1 tbsp capers

Slice the leeks across in circles very thinly (some blades on a food processor can do this for you). Place in a bowl and blanch for 2 minutes. Drain and squeeze dry. Slice the onions as thinly and mix together with the leeks. Heat the olive oil in a pan and quickly fry the almonds so that they turn golden. Pour into a bowl and add the vinegar, maple syrup, garam masala, lime zest and juice and seasoning. Mix well, then add the capers and leek mixture, toss thoroughly and serve.

❦ WARM WALNUT AND SPINACH SALAD ❦

30ml/2 tbsp walnut oil

25g/1oz ginger root, peeled and finely chopped

1 small green chilli, finely chopped

2 garlic cloves, crushed

1 bunch spring onions, trimmed

and cut in half lengthways

25g/1oz broken walnuts

450g/1lb baby spinach

5ml/1 tsp caster sugar

2.5ml/½ tsp sea salt

Heat the oil in a pan or wok and throw in the ginger root, chilli, garlic and spring onions. Stir-fry for a moment, then add the walnuts and spinach. Stir-fry for another moment (maybe 20 seconds) or until the spinach has just started to wilt. Remove from the heat, add the sugar and the salt, stir again, then empty into a serving bowl.

❦ WARM SPRING CABBAGE SALAD ❦

1 spring cabbage

55ml/2 fl oz sunflower oil

5ml/1 tsp mustard seeds

2.5ml/1/2 tsp cardamom seeds

2.5ml/1/2 tsp caraway seeds

5ml/1 tsp powdered fenugreek

1 green chilli, seeded and finely chopped

2 garlic cloves, finely chopped

sea salt (optional)

30ml/1 fl oz soy sauce

Discard any outer damaged leaves of the cabbage, then chop the inner leaves coarsely. Heat the oil in a pan and throw in the spices, chilli and garlic. Fry for a moment or until the mustard seeds begin to pop. Now add the chopped cabbage, and the salt if you're using it, and toss thoroughly. Cover the pan and leave over a low heat for 2 or 3 minutes. Pour the contents into a bowl, add the soy sauce, then toss and serve. This dish can be served with garlic croûtons (see page 4). Some good crusty bread may be needed to mop up the juices.

❧ CELERY, CARROT AND TAHINI SALAD ❧

2 celery hearts, washed and
trimmed
4 or 5 baby carrots, washed and
trimmed
few sprigs watercress, for garnish

For the sauce
30ml/2 tbsp tahini paste
10ml/2 tsp lemon juice
70ml/2½ fl oz sunflower oil
1 garlic clove, crushed
good pinch sea salt
few drops Tabasco

First make the sauce. Place the tahini in a bowl or blender and add the
lemon juice – the mixture becomes very thick. Add the oil slowly until it
becomes a smooth sauce. Add the remaining ingredients and check the
seasoning. Chop the celery into 5mm/¼ inch chunks and the carrots into
thick matchsticks. Toss the two together, then add the sauce and garnish.

❧ BROCCOLI AND AVOCADO SALAD ❧

225g/8oz broccoli
1 ripe avocado
1 packet mango strips, diced
25g/1oz pine nuts, roasted

For the dressing
45ml/3 tbsp olive oil
10ml/2 tsp lemon juice
zest of 1 lemon
10ml/2 tsp Dijon mustard
sea salt and freshly ground black
pepper

Break the broccoli into florets and plunge them into boiling water for 1
minute. Drain and refresh under cold water. Combine all the dressing
ingredients in a large bowl and dice the avocado flesh into it. Add the
broccoli, mango and pine nuts and toss carefully.

🌿 BROAD BEAN AND WALNUT SALAD 🌿

900g/2lb broad beans
85g/3oz broken walnuts
chopped green coriander, for
garnish

For the dressing
30ml/2 tbsp Plamil egg-free garlic
mayonnaise

15ml/1 tbsp lemon juice
zest of 1 lemon
45ml/3 tbsp walnut oil
2 garlic cloves, crushed
sea salt and freshly ground black
pepper

Pod the beans and boil them until tender. If the beans are old, boil for 3 minutes, leave to cool, then peel off the outer skin; this may seem a chore, but it is well worth it. How long you cook the beans depends upon their age: young broad beans need only 2–3 minutes. Make the dressing in a large bowl, add the cooked beans and broken walnuts and toss well. Garnish with the chopped coriander.

🌿 SPINACH, AVOCADO AND PEANUT SALAD 🌿

450g/1lb baby spinach, washed
and dried
1 ripe avocado
55g/2oz salted peanuts, roughly
ground

For the dressing
45ml/3 tbsp olive oil
5ml/1 tsp balsamic vinegar
sea salt and freshly ground black
pepper

Make the dressing in a large bowl. Dice the avocado into it then add the spinach leaves and toss well. Sprinkle with the ground peanuts and toss again – gently. The salad should not be disturbed too much.

🌿 RADICCHIO AND RED BEAN SALAD 🌿

Many people find radicchio lettuce too bitter for their palate, but try it with a little sugar in the dressing and with something both sharp and bland. Here, chilli and beans accompany the radicchio and make an excellent fusion of flavours.

45ml/3 tbsp olive oil
1 red chilli, finely chopped
3 garlic cloves, finely chopped
55g/2oz ginger root, peeled and grated
10ml/2 tsp caster sugar

5ml/1 tsp sea salt
1 420g/12oz tin red kidney beans, drained
1 radicchio lettuce, torn into bits
2 young carrots, grated

Heat the olive oil in a pan and stir-fry the chilli, garlic and ginger root. Stir in the sugar and salt. Remove from the heat and stir the radicchio in the oil, so that it is barely wilted. Pour the beans into a large bowl and add the oil and radicchio. Sprinkle with the grated carrot, then toss and serve.

❧ SPRING MAIN DISHES ❧

❧ POTATO AND ONION GRATIN ❧

3 large potatoes, peeled and thinly sliced

3 large onions, peeled and thinly sliced

sea salt and freshly ground black pepper

a little nutmeg

290ml/10 fl oz strong vegetable stock

30–45ml/2–3 tbsp brown breadcrumbs

Preheat the oven to 200°C/400°F/Gas mark 6. Place the potatoes in a bowl, cover with cold water and leave for 30 minutes. Drain and pat dry with a clean tea towel. Oil a shallow earthenware dish and arrange alternate layers of potato and onion, seasoning with salt, pepper and nutmeg as you go. Pour the stock over the top, sprinkle with the breadcrumbs and place in the oven for 30 minutes.

❧ SPINACH RISOTTO ❧

45ml/3 tbsp olive oil

2 garlic cloves, crushed

1 large onion, finely chopped

pinch oregano

225g/8oz arborio rice

450ml/16 fl oz strong vegetable stock

450g/1lb young spinach leaves

Heat the oil in a pan and sauté the garlic and onion for a moment or until the onion softens. Add the oregano and rice, stirring well so that the rice soaks up the oil. After 1–2 minutes, add the stock, stir again and leave to simmer, covered, over a low flame. Meanwhile, blend all the spinach into a pulp. When the risotto has cooked for 15 minutes, stir thoroughly and add the spinach pulp. Cover and simmer for another 3 minutes. Serve.

Note: I've omitted salt in this recipe as the vegetable stock might be salty enough. But all risottos seem to need a good turn of the black pepper mill.

❧ Mushroom Risotto ❧

45ml/3 tbsp olive oil
1 large onion, finely chopped
2 garlic cloves, crushed
225g/8oz field or cultivated
mushrooms, finely chopped
hefty pinch oregano
several sage leaves, finely chopped
225g/8oz arborio rice

55g/2oz dried porcini, soaked
overnight and finely chopped
450ml/16 fl oz strong vegetable
stock
sea salt and freshly ground black
pepper
45–60ml/3–4 tbsp finely chopped
coriander

Heat the oil in a pan and sauté the onion, garlic and field mushrooms for several minutes. Add the herbs, then the rice and stir until the rice has absorbed most of the flavours – about 1–2 minutes. Then add the porcini with their soaking water and the vegetable stock. Bring to a simmer, place a lid on the pan and leave over a low heat for 18 minutes. Add seasoning to taste and serve sprinkled with the coriander.

Note: Both risottos should be fairly liquid, and the rice should be al dente – still slightly chewy and nutty.

❧ Linguine con Piselli ❧

(Flat pasta noodles with a sauce made of fresh garden peas)

700g/1lb 9oz fresh garden peas
240ml/10 fl oz strong vegetable
stock
225g/8oz soya cream

sea salt and freshly ground black
pepper
5ml/1 tsp caster sugar
450g/1lb linguine, tagliatelle or
fettucine

Pod the peas, then boil the pods in the stock until soft – about 3 minutes. Blend to a purée, then sieve and reserve. Now boil the beans in a little water until tender. Drain and set aside one third of the peas. Blend the rest with the purée. Add the soya cream, seasoning and sugar.

Meanwhile, cook the pasta in lots of boiling, lightly salted water until al dente. Drain carefully and turn out into a bowl. Add the pea sauce and toss. Scatter the reserved peas over the top and serve.

🌿 PASTA WITH SPRING SAUCE 🌿

450g/1lb garden peas

sea salt and freshly ground black pepper

5ml/1 tsp caster sugar

45ml/3 tbsp olive oil

2 courgettes, diced

2 or 3 leeks, thinly sliced

1 onion, thinly sliced

3 garlic cloves, crushed

1 green chilli, sliced (optional)

bunch of watercress, chopped

450g/1lb pasta (spaghetti or what you will)

Pod the peas, then boil the pods in a little water or stock until soft. Blend to a purée, then sieve and reserve. Boil the peas in a little water until tender and blend half of them with the pod purée. Add the seasoning and sugar. Now heat the olive oil and cook the courgettes, leeks, onion, garlic and chilli until tender, about 3 minutes. Remove the pan from the heat and stir in the chopped watercress. Cook the pasta in lots of boiling, lightly salted water until al dente. Drain well and pour the pasta into a large bowl. Add the pea purée, toss thoroughly, then add the mélange of spring vegetables. Toss again and serve.

🌿 INDONESIAN RICE NOODLES 🌿

45ml/3 tbsp sesame oil

1 green chilli, finely chopped

55g/2oz ginger root, peeled and finely chopped

4 or 5 garlic cloves, finely chopped

2 or 3 spears lemon grass, trimmed and chopped

2 carrots, finely sliced

110g/4oz mushrooms, finely chopped

570ml/1 pint strong vegetable stock

2 or 3 leeks, trimmed and sliced in chunks

2 or 3 courgettes, trimmed and sliced in chunks

1 very small cauliflower, broken into florets

255g/9oz vermicelli rice noodles

zest and juice of 2 limes

sea salt and freshly ground black pepper

fresh coriander leaves, finely chopped

Heat the sesame oil in a large saucepan, throw in the chilli, ginger root and garlic and cook over a low heat for a moment. Add the lemon grass to the pan with the carrots and mushrooms. Cover and cook over a low heat for another 2 or 3 minutes. Add the stock, leeks and courgettes, cover and simmer for another 2 minutes. Add the cauliflower and cook for 2 minutes more. Now stir in the vermicelli, cover the pan and turn off the heat. Leave for 5 minutes. Stir in the lime zest and juice, taste and season. Turn out into a large tureen and sprinkle with the coriander leaves. This dish is equally good served warm or cold.

❦ SPICY GREEN INDONESIAN VEGETABLE STEW ❦

30ml/2 tbsp sesame oil
45ml/3 tbsp sunflower oil
2 green chillies, chopped
3 garlic cloves, chopped
55g/2oz ginger root, peeled and sliced into julienne strips
225g/8oz shallots, peeled
2 kohlrabi, peeled and diced
1.2 litres/2 pints strong vegetable stock
450g/1lb broad beans, podded

110g/4oz French beans, topped, tailed and broken into strips
225g/8oz asparagus, fibrous ends cut off, then cut into chunks
bunch of spring onions, trimmed and chopped
225g/8oz packet baby spinach
150ml/5 fl oz soya milk
500ml/18 fl oz tin coconut cream
sea salt and freshly ground black pepper
zest and juice of 2 limes

In a large saucepan heat the sesame and sunflower oils and throw in the chilli, garlic and ginger. Cook for a moment or two, then throw in the shallots and kohlrabi and leave to sauté for about a minute, making sure they don't stick. Pour in the stock, bring to a simmer, then add the two kinds of beans and the asparagus; cook for 3 minutes. Add the spring onions and simmer for another minute. Blend the spinach with the soya milk and add to the pan. Stir in the coconut cream, seasoning and lime juice and zest. Bring back to a simmer, then remove from the heat and allow to rest for a few minutes before giving a good stir and serving.

This dish can be eaten either with wild rice or patna rice, couscous, millet or rice noodles, or simply with good crusty bread – you need something to soak up the juices. Follow it with a mixed leaf salad to refresh the palate.

❦ WILD RICE PILAF ❦

110g/4oz wild rice
1 aubergine, trimmed and cut into
chunks
45ml/3 tbsp olive oil
2 or 3 garlic cloves, chopped
2 or 3 onions, chopped
2 small courgettes, sliced

450g/1lb tomatoes, skinned and
chopped
45ml/3 tbsp oregano
5ml/1 tsp chopped sage leaves
sea salt and freshly ground black
pepper
handful whole basil leaves
chopped parsley, for garnish

Cook the wild rice, simmering it in lightly salted water for about 45 minutes (or follow instructions on packet). Slice the aubergine into chunks. Heat the olive oil in a large pan and throw in the garlic, onions, aubergine and courgettes. Stir-fry for a minute, then add the tomatoes, oregano and sage. Cover the pan and cook for 10 minutes. When the rice is cooked, drain carefully, then tip into a bowl. Season the sauce, stir in the basil leaves then pour over the rice. Garnish with chopped parsley and serve.

🌿 SPRING SIDE DISHES 🌿

Spring vegetables are all so marvellous that they need little done to them other than steaming and serving with a little flavoured oil or chopped herbs. But there are times when you want to treat them differently, to smarten them up, to allow them to show off their quality with carefully chosen sauces and accompaniments. Do not allow anyone to be snooty about soya products: soya cream is a perfectly good ingredient to be used in cooking, and it should not be thought of as just a substitute.

🌿 BROAD BEANS WITH TOMATO, OREGANO AND BASIL SAUCE 🌿

750g/1lb 10oz broad beans
30ml/2 tbsp olive oil
2 or 3 garlic cloves, chopped
30ml/2 tbsp chopped oregano

450g/1lb tomatoes, peeled and chopped
sea salt and freshly ground black pepper
handful whole basil leaves

Pod and boil the beans until tender. Meanwhile, make the sauce. Heat the oil and throw in the garlic and oregano, then add the tomatoes and seasoning. Cover the pan and leave to simmer for 10 minutes. Drain the beans well, add to the tomato mixture and bring back to a simmer. Remove from the heat, stir in the basil leaves and serve.

🌿 BROAD BEANS WITH CREAM, CAPERS AND PARSLEY SAUCE 🌿

750g/1lb 10oz broad beans
30ml/2 tbsp walnut oil
2 or 3 shallots, sliced
100g/3½oz soya cream
45ml/3 tbsp capers

45ml/3 tbsp parsley, finely chopped
sea salt and freshly ground black pepper

Pod and boil the beans until tender. Heat the oil in a pan and cook the shallots until softened, then pour in the cream and stir thoroughly. When simmering, add the capers, parsley and seasoning. Leave to bubble for a moment before adding the drained beans and serving.

❧ POACHED SPRING ONIONS ❧

Choose plump onions with fresh green ends. Trim the white ends, chop off the green and reserve. Bring a little salted water to the boil and simmer the white ends for about 2 minutes. Add the green parts and cook for 1 minute more. Drain thoroughly and serve as a vegetable. People mistake them for baby leeks.

❧ GRATED COURGETTES WITH WALNUTS ❧

45ml/3 tbsp walnut oil

225g/8oz courgettes, trimmed and grated

zest and juice of 1 lemon

55g/2oz walnuts, crushed

5ml/1 tsp caster sugar

sea salt and freshly ground black pepper

Heat the oil, add all the ingredients and stir-fry for about half a minute, until the courgettes lose their rawness and begin to exude a little juice. Remove from the heat and serve.

❧ BABY ARTICHOKES ❧

6 to 8 baby globe artichokes

olive oil for frying

5 or 6 garlic cloves, chopped

lemon juice

sea salt

This is one of the best vegetables of spring or any other season. Trim each artichoke by tearing off the outer leaves until the inner pale green shows all around, then cut the pointed tops off. Slice the artichokes in two and dig out whatever tiny choke they might have. Heat the oil and fry the artichokes and garlic until slightly brown. Serve with the lemon juice and sea salt sprinkled over them.

❦ FRESH PEAS WITH SHREDDED LETTUCE ❦

750g/1lb 10oz fresh peas
110g/4oz baby carrots, finely
diced
30ml/2 tbsp hazelnut oil
110g/4oz shallots, peeled and
sliced

1 cos lettuce or 2 Little Gem
lettuces, sliced
5ml/1 tsp caster sugar
sea salt and freshly ground black
pepper

Cook the peas and carrots together in a little water until tender – about 3 minutes. Heat the oil in a pan and fry the shallots until softened. Add the lettuce and stir-fry for a moment until it begins to wilt. Add the drained peas and carrots, stir thoroughly, then add the sugar and seasoning.

❦ SPRING CABBAGE WITH GINGER ❦

30ml/2 tbsp olive oil
55g/2oz ginger root, peeled and
finely sliced
2 or 3 garlic cloves, diced
1 green chilli, seeded and diced
2 or 3 spring cabbages, trimmed
and chopped

15ml/1 tbsp coriander seeds,
crushed
sea salt and freshly ground black
pepper
30ml/2 tbsp chopped fresh
coriander leaves

Heat the olive oil in a wok and throw in the ginger root, garlic and chilli. Cook for a moment before adding the chopped cabbage and coriander seeds. Stir-fry for a moment, then cover and cook gently for 2–3 minutes. Add the seasoning and serve, sprinkled with the fresh coriander.

❦ AUBERGINE AND COURGETTE SLICES ❦

1 aubergine, finely sliced
2 courgettes, finely sliced

lemon juice
sea salt

Place the aubergine and courgette slices under a hot grill or on a barbecue. As soon as they begin to brown a little (within the minute), turn them over; soon after that they are done. Serve sprinkled with the lemon juice and sea salt.

❦ SPRING DESSERTS ❦

As the first green buds begin to show on the trees, rhubarb becomes available – although you can buy it forced throughout the winter. Its intense fruitiness makes it seem to me like a summer fruit and therefore to be celebrated. Here are two recipes which use it differently.

❦ RHUBARB SORBET ❦

Sorbets are wonderfully easy desserts, especially when all the soft summer and autumn berries arrive. With nearly all fruits you need to add nothing except a little sugar and perhaps some booze, though if you use too much alcohol it will not freeze. I like my sorbets to resemble granita, therefore a little soft, so leave them out of the freezer for an hour before serving. Alternatively, make them on the day required and freeze them for only 2 hours before serving.

450g/1lb rhubarb, trimmed and sliced
110g/4oz caster sugar

100ml/3½ fl oz Marsala or Madeira

Place the rhubarb in a pan with the sugar over a very low flame and leave for 15 minutes: it will cook in its own juice. Leave to cool, then place in a blender with the Marsala and blend to a purée. Freeze for a few hours.

❧ RHUBARB AND GINGER ROULADE ❧

250g/9oz frozen puff pastry,
thawed
900g/2lb rhubarb, trimmed and
cut into chunks
60ml/4 tbsp ginger marmalade
55g/2oz crystallised ginger,
chopped
30ml/2 tbsp currants
30ml/2 tbsp sultanas
45ml/3 tbsp caster sugar
soya milk, for glazing
pansy petals, for garnish

Preheat the oven to 220°C/425°F/Gas mark 7. Roll out the pastry into a rectangle. Mix the remaining ingredients, apart from the soya milk, and spread over the pastry, leaving a 2.5cm/1 inch gap around the edges. Brush the edges with the soya milk, then carefully fold the sides to the middle, pressing the edges together. Brush pastry with soya milk. Place on a baking sheet with the join beneath and bake for 20 minutes, or until puffed up and brown. Allow to rest for 10 minutes before slicing. Serve with a sauce made from equal parts of soya cream and ginger marmalade mixed together. Garnish with pansy petals.

❧ SIMPLE GRAPE PUDDING ❧

450g/1lb seedless grapes
225g/8oz tofu
225g/8oz soya cream
5ml/ tsp vanilla essence
45ml/3 tbsp muscovado sugar

Place the grapes in a shallow dish. In a blender mix the tofu with the soya cream and vanilla essence so that you have a thick sauce. Pour over the grapes and turn them so that they are covered. Sprinkle the sugar over the top and refrigerate for about 5 hours so that the sugar melts into the cream.

❦ Apricot Cream ❦

This idea came from *The Vegan Cookbook* by Alan Wakeman and Gordon Baskerville (Faber & Faber, 1986). I have simply added alcohol, which can be of any type.

200g/7oz dried apricots, finely chopped
350ml/12 fl oz soya milk

55ml/2 fl oz brandy
15ml/1 tbsp rosewater

Place all the dried apricots in a dish. Mix the remaining ingredients together and pour over them. Leave overnight. The apricots will absorb the liquid. Serve chilled.

❦ Mango Coconut Cream ❦

3 ripe mangoes
30ml/2 tbsp caster sugar

200g/7oz coconut cream

Peel the mangoes over a bowl so as not to lose any of the precious juice, then cut away as much flesh from the stone as possible. Pour the flesh and juice into a blender, add the remaining ingredients and blend to a purée. Freeze for 2 hours, so that the mixture is not frozen solid, but more like a granita.

❦ Prune Tartlets with Rum Sauce ❦

290ml/10 fl oz cold Lapsang Souchong tea
150ml/5 fl oz dark rum
225g/8oz prunes

4 individual sweet pastry cases, baked blind (see page 26)
45ml/3 tbsp muscovado sugar
geranium leaves, for garnish

Mix the tea with the rum and soak the prunes in the liquid overnight. Drain, reserving the liquid. Stone and purée the prunes and fill the pastry cases with the mixture. Place the sugar and reserved prune liquid in a saucepan and heat until the sugar caramelises a little. Spoon some of this sauce on to each plate around the tartlets. Scatter a few geranium leaves over the tartlets and serve.

🌿 Rum, Coconut and Date Cream 🌿

225g/8oz fresh dates, stoned | 200g/7oz coconut cream
110ml/4 fl oz dark rum | 30ml/2 tbsp muscovado sugar

Reserve about 6 of the dates, then blend the rest into a purée with the rum and coconut cream. Pour into a glass dish and decorate with the reserved dates. Sprinkle the sugar over the top and refrigerate for half a day or more.

🌿 Cherry Fool 🌿

900g/2lb ripe black cherries, stoned | 150ml/5 fl oz red wine
45ml/3 tbsp caster sugar | 290ml/10 fl oz soya cream or coconut cream

Place the cherries in a pan with the sugar and wine. Bring to the boil, then simmer for about 10 minutes. Leave to cool, then blend to a purée. Mix in the cream and place in a serving bowl, or individual glasses, and refrigerate for a few hours.

SUMMER

T his is the season that yields a cornucopia of produce. All the vegetables are in their prime and gluts are commonplace. Some people freeze the excess for winter use, but in our house there is never enough, and whatever the glut, everything gets eaten. It amazes me that in England people allow their French beans or mange-tout to dry out on the plant but don't pick them. The dried beans or peas inside are wonderful if blanched for an hour, then cooked in a little stock with the addition of a tablespoon of olive oil at the last moment. The small, white haricot, which is inside the French bean, is amazingly creamy and delicious. You can't find these in the supermarket, only in your own garden or allotment. Look out for the first young summer leeks. These are a great treat and should not be missed.

MENU SUGGESTIONS

Chilled Vichysoisse, Onion Filo Tart, Wilted Lettuce with Ginger, Cucumber and Peanut Salad, Strawberry Sorbet.

—

Red Pepper Cream, Three Bean Stew, Baby Carrots in Rose Mayonnaise, Warm Courgette Salad, Raspberry and Almond Tart.

—

Tomato Bliss, Spiced Potato Pie, Peas in Green Peppercorn Sauce, Celery, Endive and Aubergine Salad, Fruit Crème Brûlée.

—

Chilled Spinach and Orange Soup, Summer Tabbouleh, Leeks with Mustard Dressing, Beetroot and Ginger Salad, Summer Berry Filo Pie.

—

Chilled Mange-tout and Vodka Soup, Rice and Chickpea Pilaf, Beans in Red Pepper Sauce, Cream of Cucumber Salad, Stuffed Peaches.

—

Leek and Watercress Soup, Tofu and Bean Filo Pie, Lettuce with Black Olive Dressing, Beetroot with Coriander and Wasabi, Melon and Passion-fruit Salad.

—

Carrot and Watermelon Soup, Courgette and Bean Filo Pie, Mint and Potato Salad, Leaf Salad, Raspberry and Rose Petal Syllabub.

—

Rich Broad Bean Soup, Beetroot and Tomato Risotto, Beans in Red Pepper Sauce, Warm Courgette Salad, Gooseberry Pie.

—

❧ SUMMER SOUPS ❧

I am a devotee of iced soups, which can be both refreshing and invigorating as the beginning of a meal. They are the perfect appetiser, for they stimulate the palate without cloying it. However, soups need not be iced – they can simply be served cool at room temperature, or even warm if you prefer. Food eaten in the Mediterranean countries is always served warm rather than hot and this seems to me to be the right attitude. Flavours are dulled if food is either too hot or too cold. Remember that, if a dish is to be eaten iced, the flavours will have to be much stronger, or the dish will be bland.

For chilled dishes I find that oil is a far better fat to start cooking with, as solid fat tends to separate and looks unsightly when it resolves into tiny yellow globules. Oil simply emulsifies with the vegetable purée and makes a smooth, velvety sauce.

For the sake of tradition, I begin this section with a classic Vichysoisse because leek and potato are one of those combinations made in heaven; a leek base is also used in some of the other soups.

❧ CHILLED VICHYSOISSE ❧

30ml/2 tbsp olive oil
700g/1lb 9oz leeks, trimmed and chopped
650g/1lb 7oz floury potatoes, peeled and diced
1 litre/1¾ pints strong vegetable

stock
290ml/10 fl oz soya milk
sea salt and freshly ground black pepper
225g/8oz soya cream
handful chives, chopped

Heat the olive oil in a large saucepan and throw in the leeks and potatoes. Cook for a moment, stirring with a wooden spoon so that they don't stick, then add the vegetable stock. Bring to the boil and simmer for 20 minutes. Now add the soya milk and let the soup cool. Pour into a blender and reduce to a smooth purée. Season and add the soya cream. Refrigerate for 1 hour and serve sprinkled with the chopped chives.

✒ RED PEPPER CREAM ✒

60ml/4 tbsp olive oil

6 large red peppers, deseeded and chopped

1 red chilli

2 garlic cloves, crushed

sea salt and freshly ground black pepper

290ml/10 fl oz vegetable stock

This soup is simplicity itself to make. Heat the olive oil in a pan and throw in the peppers, chilli and garlic. Cover and leave to cook over a low heat for about 20 minutes. When the peppers are soft, leave to cool. Place the lot in a blender, season and reduce to a purée. Now add the stock and blend again.

Soups using the same recipe can also be made from green or yellow peppers.

✒ TOMATO BLISS ✒

2kg/4½lb ripe tomatoes, peeled

60ml/4 tbsp olive oil

3 garlic cloves, crushed

good pinch of sea salt

150ml/5 fl oz malt whisky

generous handful of basil leaves

Slice the peeled tomatoes in half and place them in a pan with the olive oil, garlic and salt. Cover and cook over a very low heat for 15 minutes. Leave to cool, then blend to a smooth purée. Refrigerate for 1 hour, then stir in the whisky. Float the basil leaves on top and serve.

✒ CHILLED SPINACH AND ORANGE SOUP ✒

30ml/2 tbsp olive oil

25g/1oz ginger root, peeled and finely chopped

2 garlic cloves, crushed

450g/1lb baby spinach

sea salt and freshly ground black pepper

zest and juice of 2 oranges

860ml/1½ pints vegetable stock

30ml/2 tbsp orange flower water

Heat the olive oil in a large saucepan and throw in the ginger, garlic and spinach leaves. Add a pinch of salt and the orange zest. Cover the pan and leave over a gentle heat for 5 minutes. Cool, then blend. Add the vegetable stock, then the orange juice and orange flower water. Taste and adjust seasoning, then refrigerate for 1 hour before serving.

⟨⟨ CHILLED MANGE-TOUT AND VODKA SOUP ⟩⟩

30ml/2 tbsp oil
2 garlic cloves, crushed
450g/1lb mange-tout, trimmed
pinch of sea salt

pinch of caster sugar
720ml/1¼ pints vegetable stock
110ml/4 fl oz vodka

Heat the oil in a saucepan and throw in the garlic and mange-tout. Add the salt and caster sugar and let the peas sweat for a moment or two until just soft: they should not lose their bright green colour. Remove from the heat and blend with the stock. Taste and adjust the seasoning, then add the vodka and refrigerate for 1 hour before serving.

⟨⟨ LEEK AND WATERCRESS SOUP ⟩⟩

30ml/2 tbsp olive oil
450g/1lb leeks, trimmed and sliced
pinch of sea salt

720ml/1¼ pints vegetable stock
bunch watercress, trimmed and chopped
290ml/10 fl oz soya milk

Heat the olive oil in a pan and throw in the leeks. Add the salt, cover the pan and leave to sweat over a low heat for 5 minutes. Allow to cool, then add the stock and blend. Add the watercress to the blender, followed by the soya milk. Taste and adjust the seasoning and refrigerate for 1 hour before serving.

❧ CARROT AND WATERMELON SOUP ❧

30ml/2 tbsp olive oil
450g/1lb carrots, scraped, trimmed and chopped
1 garlic clove, crushed
pinch of sea salt

pinch of caster sugar
720ml/1¼ pints vegetable stock
1 medium watermelon
geranium petals, for garnish

Heat the olive oil and throw in the carrots and garlic with the salt and sugar. Leave to sweat for a moment, then add the vegetable stock and simmer for 15 minutes. Cool, then blend. Over a large basin, so as to catch the juice, quarter the watermelon and chop it into chunks, extracting all of the black seeds as you do so. Add the juice and chunks to the carrot liquid and refrigerate the lot for 1 hour. Float some geranium petals on the soup as garnish before serving.

❧ RICH BROAD BEAN SOUP ❧

900g/2lb young broad beans
720ml/1¼ pints vegetable stock
sea salt and freshly ground black

pepper
225g/8oz soya cream
bunch of parsley, finely chopped

Pod the beans and boil them in the stock for about 5 minutes, or until tender. If there are any old beans, the outer skins must be peeled off, which is best done when they have cooled. Season the mixture, then blend the beans and stock together. Add the cream and blend again. If it is too thick, add more stock. Add the chopped parsley and refrigerate for 1 hour.

◎ SUMMER SALADS ◎

In the height of summer the most refreshing salads tend to be those made of cucumber. Tomatoes, however, are also at their best, so although they might seem commonplace, new ways of serving them feature here as well.

No daily summer diet is complete without green salads and we now have a whole range of mixed lettuce, endive and chicory leaves to choose from. There is hardly any point in giving recipes for such salads, but I would insist that you use the best extra virgin oil in the dressing and be sparing with the acidic ingredient, whether it be vinegar or lemon juice: 5ml/1 tsp to 30ml/2 tbsp of oil is a good ratio.

Delicious salads can be made out of almost any vegetable, and some, as you will see here, have been briefly cooked or seared before they are combined in the dish. Do not ignore the great range of soft fruits, for they go marvellously well with some of the vegetables.

◎ CREAM OF CUCUMBER SALAD ◎

1 whole cucumber, trimmed and sliced
sea salt
1 pink onion, trimmed and sliced
bunch chives, chopped
bunch dill, chopped
45ml/3 tbsp redcurrants

For the dressing
10ml/2 tsp red wine vinegar
10ml/2 tsp chilli oil
pinch of caster sugar
30ml/2 tbsp olive oil
30ml/2 tbsp soya cream

Arrange the sliced cucumber in a colander, sprinkle with salt and leave for 1 hour. Wash the salt away and pat the slices dry with a clean tea towel. Combine all the dressing ingredients in a large bowl. Add the onion and cucumber and toss thoroughly. Add the chives and the dill and toss again. Sprinkle over the redcurrants and serve.

◇ CUCUMBER AND PEANUT SALAD ◇

1 whole cucumber, trimmed and
diced
5ml/1 tsp salt
bunch spring onions, chopped
1 large tomato, chopped
bunch dill, chopped
55g/2oz salted peanuts, roughly
chopped

For the dressing
10ml/2 tsp red wine vinegar
10ml/2 tsp chilli oil
5ml/1 tsp maple syrup
5ml/1 tsp curry powder
15ml/1 tbsp Dijon mustard
30ml/2 tbsp olive oil

Put the diced cucumber into a bowl with the salt and leave covered for 1 hour. Drain through a colander. Make the dressing in a large bowl and add the spring onions, tomato and drained cucumber. Toss thoroughly. Add the dill, then stir in the peanuts. Serve.

◇ WARM TOMATO AND SHALLOT SALAD ◇

45ml/3 tbsp olive oil
1 red chilli, finely chopped
1 garlic clove, crushed
225g/8oz shallots, trimmed and
peeled

450g/1lb baby tomatoes (the
smaller the better)
good pinch of salt
good pinch of caster sugar
1 cos lettuce, trimmed and washed
handful of basil leaves

In a shallow pan with a lid, heat the oil and add the chilli and garlic. Throw in the shallots and cook for a moment, then add the tomatoes with the salt and the sugar. Leave to cook for about 2 minutes. The tomatoes should have split a little but they must be still whole: the shallots can still have plenty of bite in them. Arrange the lettuce leaves in a large salad bowl and pour the contents of the pan over them. Cover with the basil leaves. Before serving toss very gently.

❧ WARM COURGETTE SALAD ❧

5 or 6 small courgettes, trimmed
salt
30ml/2 tbsp olive oil
1 red chilli, finely diced
good pinch of sugar
2 or 3 large tomatoes, skinned and
chopped

1 garlic clove, crushed
1 small yellow pepper, seeded and
finely diced
good pinch of salt
45ml/3 tbsp finely chopped green
coriander

Slice each courgette lengthways into eight, place in a coriander, sprinkle with a little salt and leave for 1 hour. Wash off the salt, drain well and pat dry. Heat the oil in a wok, throw in the chilli, garlic, pepper, salt and sugar and stir-fry for about 30 seconds. Add the chopped tomatoes and stir-fry for another 20 seconds. Add the sliced courgettes, turning them in the sauce once or twice so that they just begin to cook. Remove from the heat and serve sprinkled with the coriander.

❧ CELERY, ENDIVE AND AUBERGINE SALAD ❧

2 large aubergines
45ml/3 tbsp olive oil
30ml/2 tbsp lemon juice
30ml/2 tbsp tahini paste
sea salt and freshly ground black

pepper
2 hearts of celery, chopped
2 endives, chopped
25g/1oz sultanas, soaked
overnight in dry sherry

Prick the aubergines with a fork and place in a hot oven for 1 hour. Remove, allow to cool, then scrape out all the insides. Place the flesh in a blender with the olive oil and lemon juice and blend to a purée. Add the tahini paste and seasoning and blend again to a smooth, pale cream purée. Pour the mixture into a salad bowl and add the remaining ingredients. Stir thoroughly and serve.

❧ BEETROOT AND GINGER SALAD ❧

5 or 6 small beetroots, boiled and diced
1 red pepper, seeded and diced

For the dressing
30ml/2 tbsp ginger marmalade
30ml/2 tbsp olive oil
sea salt and freshly ground black pepper

Combine all the dressing ingredients. Place the diced beetroot and pepper in a large bowl, pour in the dressing and toss.

❧ LETTUCE WITH BLACK OLIVE DRESSING ❧

12–16 black olives, stoned
45ml/3 tbsp olive oil
5ml/1 tsp lemon juice
15ml/1 tbsp capers

freshly ground black pepper
1 cos lettuce, trimmed and washed
45ml/3 tbsp blackcurrants

Throw the olives into a blender, pour in the olive oil and reduce to a purée. Add the lemon juice, then the capers and pepper. Pour into a large salad bowl. Arrange the lettuce upright around the purée. Scatter the blackcurrants over the top and serve. This salad can be tossed but to my mind it is more fun to eat if the leaves are used to scoop up the purée.

❧ MINT AND POTATO SALAD ❧

900g/2lb small new potatoes, scrubbed and boiled
1 red onion, finely chopped
bunch of spring onions, finely chopped
generous handful mint leaves, finely chopped

For the dressing
10ml/2 tsp red wine vinegar
10ml/2 tsp lemon juice
10ml/2 tsp chilli oil
2 garlic cloves, crushed
pinch of caster sugar
good pinch of sea salt
60ml/4 tbsp olive oil
30ml/2 tbsp soya cream

Slice the potatoes in half. Make the dressing and place in a large bowl. Add the potatoes and onions and toss carefully. Add the mint leaves and toss again. Serve at once.

✺ SUMMER MAIN COURSES ✺

I tend to eat lighter meals in the summer, often composed of many small dishes taken perhaps from the soups, salads and side dishes listed here. When entertaining, I like to have one large dish which acts as a centrepiece, and it is some of these that I give here. The first stew is thickened by bread, a medieval thickener, which gives a lighter quality for the summer months.

✺ THREE BEAN STEW ✺

110g/4oz flageolet beans
45ml/3 tbsp olive oil
3 garlic cloves, crushed
1 onion, chopped
15ml/1 tbsp marjoram, finely chopped
15ml/1 tbsp sage, finely chopped
1.2 litres/2 pints vegetable stock

450g/1lb broad beans, podded
225g/8oz fresh peas, podded
225g/8oz French beans, trimmed and chopped
3-day-old ciabatta loaf, diced
sea salt and freshly ground black pepper
generous handful basil leaves

Pour boiling water over the flageolets and leave to soak for 30 minutes. Heat the oil in a large saucepan and sauté the garlic and onion for a moment or two. Add the herbs followed by the drained flageolets. Leave to cook for a moment before adding the stock. Bring to the boil and simmer for 30 minutes, then add the broad beans, peas and French beans. Simmer for another 10 minutes, then add the bread and seasoning. Simmer for another 5 minutes, then turn off the heat and allow to rest for 5 minutes. Scatter basil leaves over the surface of the stew before serving.

❦ BEETROOT AND TOMATO RISOTTO ❦

45ml/3 tbsp olive oil
2 garlic cloves, crushed
1 large onion, finely chopped
pinch of oregano
225g/8oz arborio rice
450ml/16 fl oz strong vegetable
stock

450g/1lb ripe tomatoes, skinned
and chopped
2 cooked beetroots, peeled and
chopped
sea salt and freshly ground black
pepper
chopped parsley, for garnish

Heat the oil in a saucepan, throw in the garlic, onion, oregano and rice and cook for 1–2 minutes. Then add the stock, tomatoes and beetroot. Cover the pan and simmer for 18 minutes, then stir and season. Turn the heat off and leave the risotto, covered, for 3 minutes to rest. This helps the rice to expand without becoming mushy. It should remain slightly chewy. Before serving, sprinkle with chopped parsley.

✑ COURGETTE AND BEAN FILO PIE ✑

Filo pies are great for the summer months because they can be made earlier, even the day before, then reheated gently in a warm oven, or eaten at room temperature with salads. Packets of frozen filo pastry, containing 20–24 sheets, can now be bought in all supermarkets. The whole packet has to be thawed, but you can rewrap and refreeze whatever you don't use. The best tin to bake filo in is either a round, spring-clip one or a shallower tin with a loose bottom. If using the former, be sure to build up the sides with extra leaves of pastry to strengthen them.

450g/1lb broad beans, podded

45ml/3 tbsp soya cream

450g/1lb courgettes, trimmed and sliced

55ml/2 fl oz olive oil

2 garlic cloves, crushed

15ml/1 tbsp dried oregano

45ml/3 tbsp freshly chopped mint

sea salt and freshly ground black pepper

10 sheets filo pastry, thawed

Preheat the oven to 200°C/400°F/Gas mark 6. Boil the beans until tender, place them in a blender with the soya cream and reduce to a purée. Reserve. Heat 30ml/2 tablespoons of the olive oil in a pan and throw in the garlic and courgettes: fry for a few minutes, or until just softening, season and sprinkle with the oregano. Oil the baking tin with the remaining oil and line with filo pastry, sprinkling each sheet with some of the mint and oiling every third or fourth sheet (if more sheets are oiled, the pie becomes far too oily). When you have six or seven sheets making the base, pour the broad bean purée into the tin and cover with the courgettes. Tuck in the overhanging edges of filo, then cover the pie with the remaining filo, sprinkling with the last of the mint. Bake for 20 minutes, or until the top is brown and crispy.

⚛ TOFU AND BEAN FILO PIE ⚛

450g/1lb fresh peas, podded
sea salt and freshly ground black
pepper
45ml/3 tbsp soya cream
450g/1lb French beans, trimmed
and halved

55ml/2 fl oz olive oil
2 garlic cloves, crushed
225g/8oz tofu, sliced
10 sheets filo pastry, thawed
45ml/3 tbsp chopped fresh mint

Preheat the oven to 200°C/400°F/Gas mark 6. Boil the peas until cooked – a few minutes. Drain, then reduce to a purée with a little seasoning and the soya cream. Boil the French beans until tender, then drain and reserve. Heat a little of the olive oil in a pan, add the garlic and tofu and fry briefly. Make the filo base, oiling some of the sheets and sprinkling with the mint, as described in Courgette and Bean Filo Pie (page 62), then pour in the pea purée. Add the tofu and the beans. Cover with the remaining filo, sprinkle with parsley and bake for 20 minutes.

⚛ ONION FILO TART ⚛

45ml/3 tbsp olive oil
900g/2lb onions, peeled and
sliced
5ml/1 tsp sea salt
15ml/1 tbsp caster sugar
freshly ground black pepper

1.25ml/¼ tsp ground nutmeg
5ml/1 tsp juniper berries, crushed
6 sheets filo pastry, thawed
1 garlic clove, crushed
45ml/3 tbsp soya cream

Do not be put off by the amount of onions needed – the more the better, for onions reduce terrifically when cooked. Preheat the oven to 200°C/400°F/Gas mark 6. Heat 30ml/2 tbsp oil in a saucepan and cook the onions in it with the salt, sugar and spices until the onions begin to caramelise. Meanwhile, oil a flat tart tin with a removable base and line with two sheets of filo, pressing them against the sides. Combine the remaining oil with the garlic and brush over the filo. Use the remaining sheets of filo to make a strong base and sides, brushing with oil and garlic every third sheet. Fill the pastry case with baking beans and blind bake in a hot oven for 10–12 minutes. Remove the baking beans. Mix the soya cream with the cooked onions and pour into the cooked pastry case. Return to the oven and bake for another 15 minutes, or until the top is brown. Leave to cool before slicing.

❧ SPICED POTATO PIE ❧

450g/1lb new potatoes, boiled in their skins

75ml/5 tbsp olive oil

15ml/1 tbsp mustard seeds

15ml/1 tbsp grated ginger root

2 or 3 leeks, trimmed and sliced

2 or 3 onions, peeled and sliced

4 garlic cloves, crushed

1 tbsp curry powder

5ml/1 tsp sea salt

10 filo sheets, thawed

Preheat the oven to 200°C/400°F/Gas mark 6. Dice the potatoes. Heat 60ml/4 tbsp oil in a pan and throw in the mustard seeds and ginger root. Add the leeks, onions, 3 cloves of garlic, curry powder and salt and cook until the vegetables soften. Mix in the diced potato. Line an oiled baking tin with filo as described in Courgette and Bean Filo Pie (page 62). Use 15ml/1 tbsp oil mixed with 1 clove of garlic to brush over the pastry. Fill with the potato and onion mixture, cover with filo pastry and bake for 20 minutes. This pie tends to be a dry one, so serve with a sauce such as tomato coulis or the green herb sauce on page 111.

❧ SUMMER TABBOULEH ❧

110g/4oz cracked wheat or bulgur

225g/8oz fresh peas, podded

225g/8oz baby broad beans, podded

225g/8oz baby carrots, trimmed

2 or 3 tomatoes, chopped

bunch spring onions, chopped

60ml/4 tbsp chopped coriander

60ml/4 tbsp chopped mint

zest and juice of 1 lemon

75ml/5 tbsp olive oil

sea salt and freshly ground black pepper

Place the bulgur wheat in a large bowl, cover with about 2.5cm/1 inch water and leave for 30 minutes: it should soak up all the water. Transfer the bulgur to a colander and press down to extract any unwanted moisture. Boil the peas until tender, then drain and reserve. Boil the beans until tender, peeling off the inner skin if they are old. Reserve. Boil the carrots whole, then slice across thinly. In a large bowl mix the bulgur with all the vegetables, then add the herbs and dressing. Leave for 1 hour so that all the flavours are combined, then serve.

Note: If they are at hand, a few redcurrants or blackcurrants strewed over the top look and taste wonderful.

⚇ RICE AND CHICKPEA PILAF ⚇

110g/4oz chickpeas, soaked
overnight
55g/2oz wild rice
110g/4oz patna rice
2 or 3 leeks, thinly sliced and
blanched
bunch spring onions, thinly
chopped

2 fennel bulbs, trimmed and diced
60ml/4 tbsp chopped mint
zest and juice of 1 lemon
75ml/5 tbsp olive oil
sea salt and freshly ground black
pepper

Boil the chickpeas until tender – about 1 hour. Meanwhile, cook the wild rice for 40 minutes and the patna rice for about 6. Drain all three and combine in a large bowl. Add the remaining ingredients and toss thoroughly.

❧ SUMMER SIDE DISHES ❧

❧ PEAS IN GREEN PEPPERCORN SAUCE ❧

450g/lb fresh young peas, podded
60ml/4 tbsp soya cream
30ml/2 tbsp green peppercorns
30ml/2 tbsp finely chopped fresh mint

5ml/1 tsp caster sugar
5ml/1 tsp sea salt
1 red onion, finely diced, for garnish

Boil the pea pods until tender, drain and reduce to a purée in a blender. Push the liquid through a sieve, discard the fibres and reserve. Boil the peas until tender, then drain and place in bowl. Combine the soya cream and pod purée with the remaining ingredients, then pour over the peas. Garnish with the diced onion.

❧ BEANS IN RED PEPPER SAUCE ❧

30ml/2 tbsp olive oil
1 garlic clove, crushed
2 red peppers, seeded and chopped

450g/1lb broad beans
chopped fresh coriander, for garnish

Heat the oil in a saucepan and throw in the garlic and red pepper. Cover the pan and leave over a low heat for 15 minutes. Meanwhile, boil the beans until tender. Drain and remove their inner skin if old. Liquidise the red pepper mixture. Place the beans in a bowl and pour the red pepper sauce over the top. Sprinkle with the chopped coriander.

❧ GREEN PEPPERS WITH AVOCADO PURÉE ❧

4 green peppers (allow one half per person)

2 ripe avocados

45ml/3 tbsp olive oil

sea salt and freshly ground black

1 green chilli, seeded and chopped

1 garlic clove, crushed

15ml/1 tbsp lemon juice

pepper

fresh coriander leaves, for garnish

Preheat the oven to 200°C/400°F/Gas mark 6. Slice the peppers in half, discard the seeds and pith, and place the halves on a baking tray in a hot oven for 20 minutes. Meanwhile, cut the flesh from the avocados, place in a blender with the remaining ingredients and blend to a smooth, thick purée. Remove the peppers from the oven and allow to cool. Fill each half with the purée and garnish with the coriander leaves.

❧ COURGETTE MOULDS IN TOMATO COULIS ❧

450g/1lb courgettes, trimmed

650g/1lb 7oz tomatoes

30ml/2 tbsp olive oil

5ml/1 tsp sea salt

100ml/3½ fl oz fruit eau de vie

basil leaves, for garnish

Grate the courgettes into a colander, sprinkle with a very little salt, cover and leave for 1 hour. Squeeze the excess liquid from the courgettes and press them into small ramekins. Refrigerate for a few hours or a whole day. To make the coulis, chop the tomatoes and place in a saucepan with the oil and salt. Cook over a low heat for 10 minutes, then push the mixture through a sieve. Add the eau de vie and refrigerate for 1 hour. Pour a little of the coulis on each plate and carefully unmould the courgettes next to it. Decorate with a basil leaf and serve.

✂ BABY CARROTS IN ROSE MAYONNAISE ✂

450g/1lb baby carrots, trimmed
and washed
450ml/3 tbsp Plamil egg-free
garlic mayonnaise

15ml/1 tbsp rosewater
a few scented rose petals

Boil the carrots briefly so that they still have some bite in them. Mix the mayonnaise with the rosewater and pour over the drained carrots. Sprinkle with the rose petals before serving.

✂ WILTED LETTUCE WITH GINGER ✂

A good recipe for gardeners when there is a surfeit of lettuce (see also Chilled Lettuce and Melon Soup, page 31) or when they are going to seed. However, this recipe is worth making even if you have to buy the cos lettuces from the shop. Any lettuce variety will do, but the cos variety has more flavour.

2 or 3 large cos lettuces, trimmed
and outer leaves discarded
15ml/1 tbsp sesame oil
30ml/2 tbsp olive oil
1 garlic clove, crushed
1 green chilli, seeded and finely

chopped
55g/2oz root ginger, peeled and
cut into julienne strips
sea salt
5ml/1 tsp caster sugar
15ml/1 tbsp pickled ginger pieces

Tear the lettuce into individual leaves. Heat the two oils in a wok, throw in the garlic, chilli and ginger and stir-fry for a moment. Add the lettuce and stir-fry until the leaves begin to wilt, then add the salt and sugar. Toss thoroughly, throw in the pickled ginger and serve.

⚡ LEEKS WITH MUSTARD DRESSING ⚡

about 10 small leeks, trimmed, white parts only

For the dressing
15ml/1 tbsp lemon juice

good pinch of sea salt
good pinch of caster sugar
15ml/1 tbsp Dijon mustard
45ml/3 tbsp olive oil
45ml/3 tbsp soya cream

Steam the leeks for 8–10 minutes or until tender: there should be still some bite in them. Drain the leeks well and place in serving dish. Mix all the dressing ingredients together and, when thick and creamy, pour over the leeks and serve.

⚡ BEETROOT WITH CORIANDER AND WASABI ⚡

Wasabi is a Japanese horseradish which you can buy in powder form in Western health and wholefood shops. In Japanese restaurants it appears as a tiny green cone alongside a dish of tempura or sushi, and is used as a dip. The powder needs to be made up with water and left for at least 15 minutes before the full aromatic, fiery essence is released.

6 or 8 beetroot, boiled and peeled

For the dressing
5ml/1 tsp wasabi powder
good pinch of caster sugar
45ml/3 tbsp olive oil

5ml/1 tsp coriander seeds, finely ground
15ml/1 tbsp lemon juice
good pinch of sea salt
45ml/3 tbsp soya cream
a few geranium petals, for garnish

First make the wasabi paste by adding a little water to the wasabi powder and leaving it for 15 minutes. Mix together the other dressing ingredients, add the wasabi and leave for another 15 minutes. Slice or dice the beetroot and arrange on a plate. Pour the dressing over and scatter the geranium petals on top.

❧ SUMMER PUDDINGS ❧

❧ MELON AND PASSION-FRUIT SALAD ❧

juice of 3 oranges and the zest of 1
30ml/2 tbsp orange flower water
110g/4oz caster sugar
55g/2oz sultanas

55g/2oz candied lemon peel
1 ripe Charentais or Ogen melon, deseeded
6 passion-fruit
55ml/2 fl oz fruit eau de vie

Heat the orange juice, zest and the orange flower water in a saucepan with the sugar until the sugar dissolves. Throw in the sultanas, the candied peel and the eau de vie. Leave to steep for 30 minutes. Cut the melon flesh into chunks and place in a bowl. Slice the top of each passion-fruit and dig out all the seeds and juice with a spoon. Pour over the melon with the orange sauce, add the eau de vie and toss gently. Refrigerate and serve.

❧ STRAWBERRY SORBET ❧

225g/8oz strawberries
30ml/2 tbsp caster sugar
55ml/2 fl oz eau de vie

geranium or viola petals, for garnish

Place the strawberries, sugar and eau de vie in a blender and blend to a purée. Freeze the mixture but take out 1 hour before serving: it should be the consistency of a granita, not frozen solid. Decorate with a few hulled strawberries and some geranium or viola petals.

A salad of mixed leaves and flowers. Flowers have distinct and different flavours – so enjoy them.

Gazpacho – scatter finely chopped cucumber and red pepper on this highly refreshing chilled soup.

As a first course make individual Tomato Tarts.

The distinct flavour of globe artichokes in this Artichoke, Potato and Carrot Stew will permeate the whole dish.

Potato and Onion Gratin, dusted with grated nutmeg – a classic combination.

Spicey Fried Cauliflower should have plenty of bite in it, served here with chutneys and steamed spinach.

Apricot Tart – glowing with golden fruit, a wonderful way to finish a meal.

Sussex Pond Pudding – the deceptively plain exterior hides its tangy, rich lemon centre.

Strawberry Sorbet – serve with frozen and fresh strawberries for a delightful combination of textures.

✺ RASPBERRY AND ALMOND TART ✺

1 baked sweet pastry case (see
Apricot Tart, page 24)
450g/1lb raspberries
110g/4oz ground almonds
225g/8oz soya cream

2 tbsp caster sugar
90ml/6 tbsp raspberry jam
25g/1oz flaked almonds
a little icing sugar

Preheat the oven to 200°C/400°F/Gas mark 6. Blend half the raspberries to a purée and mix with the ground almonds, the soya cream and most of the sugar. Smear the bottom of the pastry case with half the raspberry jam. Melt the remainder of the jam. Pour the raspberry purée into the pastry case and bake for about 20 minutes. When it is cool, cover with the remaining melted jam and then the remaining raspberries and flaked almonds. Dust with icing sugar and serve.

✺ SUMMER BERRY FILO PIE ✺

60ml/4 tbsp vegetable fat
pinch of cinnamon
pinch of mixed spice
30ml/2 tbsp caster sugar

12 sheets filo pastry, thawed
450g/1lb mixed blackcurrants and
redcurrants
60–75ml/4–5 tbsp maple syrup

Preheat the oven to 200°C/400°F/Gas mark 6. Melt the vegetable fat in a saucepan with the spices and the sugar. Grease a tart tin and line it with a sheet of filo pastry. Brush with a little spiced fat, then place another sheet on top and brush that with the fat too. Scatter a few currants over the pastry, dribble 15ml/1 tablespoon of maple syrup over the top, then cover with another filo sheet. Continue building up the layers of filo, currants and maple syrup until you have only two sheets left. Press these sheets gently over the top, brush with more fat and bake for 20 minutes, or until brown and crisp. Pour a little more maple syrup over the top and leave to cool before slicing.

✄ STUFFED PEACHES ✄

4 peaches (allow 1 per person)
60ml/4 tbsp ground almonds
30ml/2 tbsp chopped almonds
30ml/2 tbsp candied lemon peel,
chopped

30ml/2 tbsp caster sugar
45ml/3 tbsp lemon or grapefruit
marmalade
75ml/5 tbsp white wine

Preheat the oven to 180°C/350°F/Gas mark 4. Blanch the peaches for a moment so that the skins will slip off, then cut the fruit in half and remove the stones. Mix everything else together, except the wine, and fill the stone cavity with the stuffing. Lay the peaches on a baking sheet and pour the wine around them. Bake in the oven for 20 minutes. Serve warm.

✄ RASPBERRY AND ROSE PETAL SYLLABUB ✄

225g/8oz tofu
450g/1lb soya cream
450g/1lb raspberries

30ml/2 tbsp caster sugar
petals of 1 perfumed rose, chopped

Beat the tofu into the cream. Blend two-thirds of the raspberries and add with the sugar to the cream. Stir in the rose petals followed by the whole raspberries. Refrigerate for a few hours. Serve with a garnish of more rose petals.

✄ GOOSEBERRY PIE ✄

450g/1lb gooseberries, topped
and tailed
30ml/2 tbsp caster sugar

110ml/4 fl oz dry sherry
110g/4oz sweet pastry (see
page 24)
soya milk, for glazing

Preheat the oven to 200°C/400°F/Gas mark 6. Throw the gooseberries into a deep pie dish, sprinkle the sugar over them and then pour in the sherry. Roll out the pastry to fit the top of the dish. Trim to size, cut a cross in the middle and glaze with soya milk. Bake for 20–30 minutes, or until the inside has bubbled up and the pastry is brown.

❧ Fruit Crème Brûlée ❧

900g/2lb fruit in season, such as
white and black seedless grapes,
blueberries, strawberries,

redcurrants or blackcurrants
225g/8oz soya cream
30ml/2 tbsp muscovado sugar

Preheat the grill to very hot. Remove all the stalks from the fruit, then spread out the fruit in a shallow dish that will fit neatly beneath the grill. Pour the soya cream over the top so that all the fruit is covered. Sprinkle the muscovado sugar on top of the cream. Place the dish under the preheated grill for 10–15 seconds, or until the sugar has melted and is bubbling. Serve at once.

AUTUMN

Autumn is renowned for some of the most delicious fruits of the earth. For a start there are mushrooms and fungi – yes, I know you can now get many of them all year round, but the flavour and quality of wild mushrooms picked at this time of year takes some beating. Then there are two great foods from the New World, sweetcorn and pumpkins; both make marvellous soups, starters and side dishes. Lastly there are new green flageolets (also originally from the New World, as they are haricots, but now associated with France and its cuisine), the praise of which I sing below. Autumn is also the season of peppers, fennel, endive and chicory, beetroot, blackberries, apples and pears. It is a good time, for like the spring, autumn's fruits seem to taste more intensely, as if the plant knows it has reached the end of another cycle and is determined to give its all.

MENU SUGGESTIONS

Clear Mushroom Soup, Tomato Tart, Glazed Turnips, Carrot, Almond and Rose Salad, Plum Crumble.	Tempeh and Mushroom, Broccoli Purée with Pine Nuts, Beetroot and Ginger Salad, Baked Figs.	Purée, Bean and Avocado Flan, Stuffed Mushrooms, Rocket and Radicchio Salad, Damson Cream.	Pumpkin and Ginger Soup, Potato, Sweetcorn and Mushroom Gratin, Endive with Avocado and Watercress Cream, Leaf Salad, Stuffed Pancakes.
—	—	—	
Black Mushroom Soup, Leek Feuillette, Roasted Parsnips, Flageolet Salad, Chestnut Cream.	Flageolet and Sweetcorn Soup, Potato and Mushroom Pie, Fried Spicy Cauliflower, Bean and Caramelised Onion Salad, Apple Fritters	Pumpkin Soup, Onion and Parsnip Gratin, Indonesian Mushroom Salad, Sweetcorn and Apple Salad, Marinated Peaches.	—
			Ratatouille Soup, Cream of Flageolet Tart, Greek Mushroom Salad, Tomato and Basil Salad, Caramel Apple Slices.
—	—	—	
Flageolet Soup, Roulade of	Sweetcorn Soup with Red Pepper		

❧ AUTUMN SOUPS ❧

❧ CLEAR MUSHROOM SOUP ❧

5ml/1 tbsp sesame oil
25g/1oz ginger root, peeled and sliced into julienne strips
2 garlic cloves, crushed
green chilli, seeded and diced
225g/8oz mushrooms, washed and thinly sliced
5 or 6 spring onions, trimmed and chopped into 2.5cm/1 inch lengths

1.2 litres/2 pints strong vegetable stock
zest and juice of 2 limes
10ml/2 tsp mushroom essence
sea salt and freshly ground black pepper
100ml/3½ fl oz dry sherry
30ml/2 tbsp chopped green coriander

Heat the sesame oil in a saucepan, throw in the ginger, garlic and chilli, followed by the mushrooms and spring onions, and sauté for 1 minute, stirring, over a low heat. Add the vegetable stock, bring to the boil and simmer for 5 minutes. Stir in the lime zest and juice and the mushroom essence. Bring back to the boil then remove from the heat and leave to rest for 5 minutes. Taste and check for seasoning. Add the sherry and serve with the coriander floating on the surface.

❧ BLACK MUSHROOM SOUP ❧

30ml/2 tbsp olive oil
2 onions, trimmed and chopped
2 garlic cloves, crushed
225g/8oz field mushrooms, chopped
2 bay leaves

1.2 litres/2 pints vegetable stock
225g/8oz soya cream
sea salt and freshly ground black pepper
100ml/3½ fl oz dark sherry, Madeira or Marsala

Heat the oil in a large saucepan and throw in the onions, garlic and mushrooms with the bay leaves. Place over a low heat, cover the pan and cook slowly for 10 minutes. Pour in the vegetable stock, leave to cool, take out the bay leaves, then liquidise the lot. Add the soya cream and taste for seasoning. Add the sherry and serve.

❋ FLAGEOLET SOUP ❋

If you are lucky enough to find fresh flageolets at this time of year, buy them immediately. French markets south of Paris have them in September and October, still in their pods. The heaps of dry white husks hold creamy, apple green beans of an astoundingly rich flavour. In Britain I have grown them successfully in my own garden. If only British farmers would cultivate them.

The dried flageolets you can buy in supermarkets are probably a year old, maybe more. These are the next best thing to the freshly dried variety, but they need 40 minutes' cooking compared to only 10 or 15 minutes. This recipe is for flageolets you are likely to find in the shops. Fresh flageolets need no soaking.

30ml/2 tbsp olive oil

1 onion, chopped

2 garlic cloves, crushed

110g/4oz flageolets, soaked for 1 hour

1.75 litres/3 pints vegetable stock

sea salt and freshly ground black pepper

45ml/3 tbsp chopped parsley

Heat the oil in a saucepan, throw in the onion and garlic and leave to sweat for a moment or two. Add the drained flageolets and vegetable stock. Bring to the boil and simmer for 40–45 minutes, when the beans should be soft. Cool and liquidise to a smooth purée. Taste for seasoning, reheat gently and add the parsley before serving.

❋ FLAGEOLET AND SWEETCORN SOUP ❋

45ml/3 tbsp olive oil

1 onion, chopped

2 garlic cloves, crushed

1 red chilli, seeded and chopped

3 carrots, finely diced

110g/4oz flageolets, soaked for 1 hour

1.75 litres/3 pints vegetable stock

3 corn on the cob, boiled and kernels cut out

sea salt and freshly ground black pepper

45ml/3 tbsp green onion, finely chopped

Heat the oil in a large saucepan, throw in the onion, garlic, chilli and carrots and sauté for a moment. Add the drained flageolets and cook briefly before adding the stock. Simmer for 40 minutes, then add the corn and simmer for another 5 minutes. Taste for seasoning then add the chopped green onion and serve.

❋ SWEETCORN SOUP WITH RED PEPPER PURÉE ❋

45ml/3 tbsp olive oil

1 onion, chopped
chopped

3 corn on the cob, boiled and
kernels cut out

1.75 litres/3 pints vegetable stock

2 garlic cloves, crushed

4 red peppers, seeded and
chopped

sea salt and freshly ground black
pepper

225g/8oz soya cream

Heat the olive oil in a pan and throw in the onion, garlic and red peppers. Cover and leave to cook over a low heat for 20 minutes. When soft, leave to cool, then blend to a thick purée. Taste to check seasoning, then reserve. Now blend the corn with the vegetable stock, check the seasoning, then add the soya cream. To serve, reheat the corn soup and pepper purée separately. Pour the soup into individual bowls and pour a swirl of the purée into the centre of each.

❋ PUMPKIN SOUP ❋

This is one of the best autumnal soups and a simple classic.

60ml/4 tbsp olive oil

1 onion, finely chopped

2 garlic cloves, crushed

450g/1lb pumpkin flesh, peeled
and cubed

sea salt and freshly ground black
pepper

720ml/1¼ pints vegetable stock

red geranium petals, for garnish

Heat the olive oil and throw in the onion, garlic and pumpkin flesh. Add sea salt and a little black pepper. Cover the pan and leave over a gentle heat for 15 minutes. Now add the vegetable stock and simmer for 5 minutes. Leave to cool, then blend; this will give you a thick, golden purée. Add more stock if you want a thinner soup. Reheat gently and sprinkle with the geranium petals before serving.

❋ PUMPKIN AND GINGER SOUP ❋

60ml/4 tbsp olive oil
1 onion, finely chopped
2 garlic cloves, crushed
55g/2oz ginger root, peeled and
cut into julienne strips
1 red chilli, seeded and diced
225g/8oz pumpkin flesh, peeled
and cubed

1.2 litres/2 pints vegetable stock
sea salt and freshly ground black
pepper
30ml/2 tbsp pickled ginger, finely
diced
30ml/2 tbsp finely chopped
parsley

Heat the olive oil in a saucepan and throw in the onion, garlic, ginger root, chilli and pumpkin. Cover the pan and leave to cook gently over a low heat for 20 minutes. Take half the mixture and liquidise it, then pour it back into the pan with the rest of the soup. Add the vegetable stock and seasoning. Bring to the boil and simmer for 5 minutes. Sprinkle the pickled ginger and parsley over the top of the soup before serving.

❋ RATATOUILLE SOUP ❋

60ml/4 tbsp olive oil
1 aubergine, chopped
2 red peppers, seeded and
chopped
2 green peppers, seeded and
chopped
2 or 3 courgettes, trimmed and
sliced
2 onions, peeled and chopped

2 garlic cloves, crushed
900g/2lb tomatoes, skinned and
chopped
15ml/1 tbsp oregano
sea salt and freshly ground black
pepper
720ml/1¼ pints vegetable stock
45ml/3 tbsp chopped parsley

Heat the olive oil in a large saucepan and throw in all the chopped vegetables with the oregano and seasoning. Cover the pan and leave to simmer over a low heat for 30–40 minutes. Pour half the soup into a blender and liquidise, then pour it back in the pan. Add the vegetable stock and bring to a simmer, stirring. Check the seasoning, throw in the chopped parsley and serve.

❧ AUTUMN SALADS ❧

❧ GREEK MUSHROOM SALAD ❧

45ml/3 tbsp olive oil
2 garlic cloves, crushed
5ml/1 tsp coriander seeds, freshly ground
5ml/1 tsp mustard seeds
2 or 3 bay leaves

225g/8oz flat mushrooms, trimmed and broken up
zest and juice of 1 lemon
sea salt and freshly ground black pepper
flat leaf parsley, chopped

Heat the olive oil in a shallow pan, throw in the garlic, spices and bay leaves, then add the mushrooms. Fry gently turning the mushrooms in the spices. Add the lemon zest and fry for another moment. When the mushrooms are cooked, add the lemon juice, seasoning and parsley. Leave to cool. This is delicious eaten cold with good crusty bread.

❧ INDONESIAN MUSHROOM SALAD ❧

15ml/1 tbsp sesame oil
15ml/1 tbsp peanut oil
55g/2oz ginger root, peeled and cut into julienne strips
1 red chilli, diced
3 garlic cloves, chopped
2 spears lemon grass, trimmed and chopped
110g/4oz cultivated mushrooms, trimmed and sliced

110g/4oz oyster mushrooms, broken up
110g/4oz flat mushrooms, trimmed and sliced
zest and juice of 2 limes
sea salt and freshly ground black pepper
45ml/3 tbsp green coriander, finely chopped

Heat the oils in a shallow pan and throw in the ginger, chilli, garlic and lemon grass, followed by the mushrooms. Fry gently for about 15 minutes. Add the remaining ingredients and serve hot or cold.

❧ FLAGEOLET SALAD ❧

225g/8oz flageolet beans, soaked
for 1 hour
60ml/4 tbsp olive oil
1 onion, peeled and chopped
1 green chilli, seeded and chopped
2 garlic cloves, crushed
30ml/2 tbsp green peppercorns

zest of 1 lemon
30ml/2 tbsp lemon juice
bunch spring onions, finely
chopped
sea salt and freshly ground black
pepper

Boil the flageolets for about 40 minutes, or until they are tender. Drain well and reserve. Meanwhile, heat the olive oil in a pan and fry the onion, chilli and garlic for a moment. Remove from the heat and add the peppercorns, lemon zest and juice. Pour the beans into a large bowl, add the spring onions and toss well. Add the onion mixture and seasoning, toss again and leave for 1 hour so the beans soak up all the flavours.

❧ SWEETCORN AND APPLE SALAD ❧

15ml/1 tbsp lemon juice
45ml/3 tbsp olive oil
15ml/1 tbsp Dijon mustard
sea salt and freshly ground black
pepper
4 corn on the cob, boiled and

kernels cut out
4 dessert apples, peeled, cored
and sliced
55g/2oz raisins, soaked in sherry
overnight
55g/2oz pine nuts, roasted

In a large bowl mix together the lemon juice, oil, mustard and seasoning, then add the rest of the ingredients. Toss thoroughly and leave for 1 hour before serving.

Bean and Caramelised Onion Salad

30ml/2 tbsp olive oil
4 or 5 onions, peeled and sliced
10ml/2 tsp caster sugar
5ml/1 tsp sea salt
1 kg/2¼lb French beans, trimmed
30ml/2 tbsp lemon juice
2 tbsp cashew nuts, roughly ground

Heat the oil in a pan and throw in the onions, sugar and salt. Cover the pan and leave over a gentle heat for 30–40 minutes, or until the onions have all partially caramelised. During the last 10 minutes, boil the beans until just tender. Drain well and keep warm. Remove the onions from the heat and stir in the lemon juice. Pour the beans into a bowl, add the onion mixture and toss thoroughly. Sprinkle with the cashew nuts before serving.

Rocket and Radicchio Salad

Radicchio is mostly eaten raw in leaf salads and, one suspects, is usually included for its bright magenta colour rather than its flavour. In this recipe the radicchio is stir-fried, and therefore partially wilted, so some of the bright red changes to green. This also makes the flavour less bitter and is an agreeable foil to the peppery rocket. I believe the flavour of rocket is far superior when the leaves are untouched by any dressing, which goes some way to explain the method of this recipe.

30ml/2 tbsp sesame oil
2 heads radicchio, torn into separate leaves
10ml/2 tsp caster sugar
5ml/1 tsp sea salt
large bunch of rocket

Heat the sesame oil in a wok, throw in the radicchio leaves, sugar and salt and stir-fry for a moment or two. When half the leaves are wilted and have turned dark green, remove from the heat and transfer to a salad bowl. Add the rocket leaves, toss and serve.

❧ ENDIVE WITH AVOCADO AND WATERCRESS CREAM ❧

2 bunches watercress, most of their
stalks removed
2 ripe avocados, peeled and
stoned
30ml/2 tbsp lemon juice
zest of 1 lemon

1 garlic clove, crushed
60ml/4 tbsp olive oil
sea salt and freshly ground black
pepper
2 or 3 endives, separated into
leaves

Roughly chop the watercress, place it in a blender and reduce to a pulp. Add the avocado flesh with the lemon juice and zest, garlic, oil and seasoning and blend to a smooth, vivid green purée. Pour into a bowl and use the endive leaves as scoops for the purée.

❧ TOMATO AND BASIL SALAD ❧

No autumn can be complete without this classic. But if this dish is to be at its peak, the tomatoes should be *marmande* and purchased in a Mediterranean country: better still, they should be gathered from the plant while still warm from the sun. Likewise the basil, olives, capers and onions should all be home-grown, and the oil must be extra virgin. The dish is a rustic homily to Mediterranean peasant culture. It is simple and bursting with flavours and is almost impossible for us to reproduce from supermarket ingredients. Nevertheless, our crude attempt at perfection can also be highly edible.

900g/2lb large, ripe tomatoes,
trimmed and sliced in rounds
2 or 3 pink onions, sliced in thin
circles
45ml/3 tbsp black olives, stoned
300ml/2 tbsp capers

10ml/2 tsp red wine vinegar
60ml/4 tbsp olive oil
sea salt and freshly ground black
pepper
large bunch basil leaves

Arrange the tomato slices on a large platter, cover with the pink onion, then dot the olives and capers over the top. Mix together the vinegar, oil and seasoning and pour over the salad. Roughly tear up the basil leaves, scatter over the lot and serve.

✽ AUTUMN
MAIN DISHES ✽

Pastry made with margarine is spurned by gourmets and food writers, for eating the best pastry is one of those indelible experiences – crumbly, flaky, buttery, lingering on the palate, both rich and featherlight. It seems as singular as a piece of music that refuses to go away. So before I experimented with pastry which used no butter, egg yolks (or crème fraîche which I used always for tarte tatin), I admit I was worried: I recalled too well the best pastry I ever made, which I believe was superb because of the purity of the ingredients – unpasteurised butter, stoneground flour and spring water. The last two can be managed easily enough, but the flavour of the fat used is what gives pastry its fine taste and texture. However, there are ways in which some of the buttery richness can be suggested: a tablespoon or more of soya flour mixed in with the stoneground flour helps, as soya has the richness of egg yolk and gives a crumbly texture to the cooked pastry; a little lemon juice helps to break down the gluten in the flour. Of the fats, you must decide what suits you. There is a range to choose from, some specifically made for pastry-making. For some dishes you can use an olive oil pastry, but this has to be rolled out between two sheets of cling film or it breaks up. Soya cream makes an adequate substitute for crème fraîche in some pastry.

Note: Shop-bought frozen pastry, both shortcrust and puff, is made from margarine, so is acceptable in this book. Note, however, that some luxury varieties are made from butter, so check the ingredients list. Home-made puff pastry needs plenty of time and the skills of a *patissier*, which very few of us have.* Two recipes below specify bought puff pastry, which can give gratifying results.

* If you want to learn pastry skills, consult *Leith's Book of Baking* by Prue Leith and Caroline Waldegrave (Bloomsbury, 1993).

❋ BASIC PASTRY RECIPE ❋

200g/7oz white stoneground flour   overnight

25g/1oz soya flour   30ml/1 tbsp lemon juice

pinch each of salt and sugar   a little cold water

110g/4oz vegetable fat, frozen

Mix the two flours together, adding the salt and sugar. Grate the fat into the flour, then mix thoroughly with your fingers to the texture of fine breadcrumbs. Add the lemon juice and enough cold water to make a dough: too much water gives a hard, brittle pastry, and too little means the pastry will fall apart. Roll the dough into a ball, cover with grease-proof paper and refrigerate for 1 hour. Remove from the refrigerator and leave for 10 minutes at room temperature before rolling out. This quantity of pastry will line a 20cm/8 inch × 2.5cm/1 inch tin or a 25cm/10 inch × 1cm/½ inch tin.

To bake blind: Preheat the oven to 220°C/425°F/Gas mark 7. Line a tart or pie tin with the rolled-out pastry, fitting it snugly around the sides. Trim the edges, then prick the base with a fork. Line the pastry case with aluminium foil. Cover the foil evenly with baking beans and bake for 10 minutes. Remove from the oven, lift out the foil and beans, then leave the case for a further 2–3 minutes so that the base dries out. Remove from the oven and use right away, or keep in the refrigerator for a couple of days before using.

❋ TOMATO TART ❋

20cm/8 inch × 2.5cm/1 inch pastry case, baked blind (see above)   2 onions, peeled and sliced

about 6 tomatoes, peeled and sliced   12 black olives, stoned and halved

bunch of basil leaves

sea salt and freshly ground black pepper

Preheat the oven to 220°C/425°F/Gas mark 7. Fill the pastry case with a layer of tomatoes followed by a layer of onions. Season, dot with some of the olives and arrange a few basil leaves on top. Continue with the layers, pressing down gently and filling as tightly as possible. Finish with a layer of tomatoes. Bake for 15–20 minutes, when the top should be crisp.

Note: The layers will sink as they cook. Once cooled, the tart can have its sides trimmed if you wish.

❧ CREAM OF FLAGEOLET TART ❧

30ml/2 tbsp olive oil
1 onion, finely chopped
2 garlic cloves, crushed
15ml/1 tbsp oregano
170g/6oz flageolet beans, soaked
sea salt and freshly ground black
pepper

for 1 hour
720ml/1¼ pints vegetable stock
2 bay leaves
225g/8oz soya cream
45ml/3 tbsp chopped parsley
25cm/10 inch × 1cm/½ inch
pastry case, baked blind (see page
84)

Heat the oil in a saucepan, throw in the onion, garlic and oregano and cook gently until the onion begins to soften. Add the drained flageolets and the vegetable stock. The liquid should cover the beans by about 2.5cm/1 inch; if not, add more water or stock. Add the bay leaves, bring to the boil and simmer for 30–40 minutes, when all the stock should have been absorbed and the beans are tender. If the liquid is gone before the beans are cooked, add more stock. If the beans are done but some liquid remains, drain it away. Preheat the oven to 220°C/425°F/Gas mark 7. Add the cream, parsley and seasoning to the bean mixture. Bring to the boil and pour into the pastry case. Bake for 20 minutes and leave for a good few hours before slicing.

* BEAN AND AVOCADO FLAN *

450g/1lb French beans, trimmed and boiled

2 garlic cloves, crushed

1 green chilli, seeded and diced

sea salt and freshly ground black pepper

45ml/3 tbsp soya cream

30cm/12 inch × 1cm/½ inch pastry case, baked blind (see page 84)

1 ripe avocado

a few black olives, stoned

Preheat the oven to 220°C/425°F/Gas mark 7. Drain the beans well, reserve about ten of them and place the rest in a blender with the garlic, chilli seasoning and soya cream. Blend to a thick purée, pour into the pastry case and spread it carefully over the base. Bake for 10–12 minutes. Remove from the oven, allow to rest for 5 minutes, then use the reserved beans to make a lattice pattern, pressing them gently into the surface. Peel the avocado, slice in two and discard the stone. Place the two halves together and slice across in rounds. Fit the rounds in the middle of each lattice square, pressing down gently. Place half an olive in the middle of each avocado circle. Serve at once.

Note: This flan will not keep, as the exposed avocado will turn black. To avoid this you can use sliced tomato instead.

✳ ROULADE OF TEMPEH AND MUSHROOM ✳

45ml/3 tbsp olive oil

3 garlic cloves, crushed

1 green chilli, seeded and diced

225g/8oz tempeh, thawed and cubed

225g/8oz mushrooms, trimmed and sliced

110g/4oz potato, boiled, seasoned and mashed with olive oil

75ml/5 tbsp finely chopped parsley

4 or 5 spring onions, finely chopped

sea salt and freshly ground black pepper

225g/8oz frozen puff pastry, thawed

15ml/1 tbsp soya milk

15ml/1 tbsp sesame seeds

Preheat the oven to 220°C/425°F/Gas mark 7. Heat the olive oil in a pan and throw in the garlic, chilli, tempeh and mushrooms. Fry for about 5 minutes or until the mushrooms have cooked and the tempeh has become brown and crisp. Pour the mixture into a bowl, add the potato, parsley, onions and seasoning and mix thoroughly. Now roll out the puff pastry into a rectangle about 30cm/12 inches × 40cm/16 inches. Spread the mushroom mixture over the pastry, leaving 1cm/½ inch margin around the edges. Starting at the narrow edge, carefully roll up the pastry and place in an oiled baking tin, seam side down. Brush with a little soya milk and sprinkle with sesame seeds. Bake for 30 minutes, or until puffed up and brown. Let the roulade rest for 5 minutes before carefully slicing it across. Serve with the red pepper purée (page 77), the green herb sauce (page 111) or the black olive sauce (page 111).

❋ LEEK FEUILLETTE ❋

225g/8oz frozen puff pastry, thawed

8 small leeks, trimmed to about 23cm/5 inches long

90ml/6 tbsp soya cream

45ml/3 tbsp green peppercorns

30ml/2 tbsp finely chopped parsley

sea salt and freshly ground black pepper

Preheat the oven to 220°C/425°F/Gas mark 7. Roll out the pastry to a thickness of 2.5m/¼ inch. Using a sharp knife, cut eight strips measuring 5 cm/2 inches wide × 15cm/6 inches long. On four of the strips mark the pastry with three slashes; on the other four, mark a rectangle large enough to hold two leeks. Place the pastry strips on a baking tray and bake for about 12 minutes. Meanwhile, steam the leeks for about 5 minutes. In a bowl combine the soya cream with the peppercorns, parsley and seasoning. Remove the pastry strips from the oven and carefully extract the marked out inner rectangles. Fit the leeks in the cavities and pour a little sauce over them. Fit a pastry 'lid' over the top and replace in the preheated oven to warm for a few minutes.

❋ AUTUMN CASSEROLE ❋

45ml/3 tbsp olive oil

3 garlic cloves, crushed

1 green chilli, seeded and diced

225g/8oz mushrooms, sliced

110g/4oz haricot beans, blanched and soaked for 1 hour

55g/2oz porcini, blanched and soaked for 1 hour

720ml/1¼ pints vegetable stock

1.35kg/3lb tomatoes, skinned and chopped

3 corn on the cob, boiled and kernels cut out

sea salt and freshly ground black pepper

45ml/3 tbsp chopped parsley

Heat the oil in a large saucepan, throw in the garlic, chilli and mushrooms and leave to sweat for a moment or two. Add the beans and porcini with their soaking liquid. Pour in the vegetable stock, bring to the boil and simmer for 30 minutes. Now add the chopped tomatoes and simmer for another 15 minutes. Add the corn and simmer for a further 5 minutes. Taste and check for seasoning. Pour into a tureen, sprinkle the parsley over the top and serve.

❋ POTATO AND MUSHROOM PIE ❋

60ml/4 tbsp olive oil

1 red chilli, seeded and finely diced

2 garlic cloves, crushed

450g/1lb mushrooms, trimmed and sliced

1 red pepper, seeded and finely diced

2 large tomatoes, peeled and chopped

45ml/3 tbsp shoyu or soy sauce

45ml/3 tbsp vegetable stock

700g/1lb 9oz potatoes, peeled and boiled

2 onions, finely chopped

75ml/5 tbsp finely chopped parsley

sea salt and freshly ground black pepper

60ml/4 tbsp soya cream

Preheat the oven to 200°C/400°F/Gas mark 6. Heat the oil in a frying pan and throw in the chilli and garlic, followed by the mushrooms and red pepper. Cook for about 5 minutes, stirring frequently, then add the tomatoes and cook for another 5 minutes. Mix the soy sauce and stock together, pour over the mushroom mixture and bring to the boil. Transfer to a shallow pie dish. Now mash the potatoes with the remaining ingredients and spread over the mushrooms. Bake for about 30 minutes.

❀ POTATO, SWEETCORN AND MUSHROOM GRATIN ❀

This uses a similar mixture to the recipe above, but includes a more exotic selection of mushrooms.

60ml/4 tbsp olive oil
1 red chilli, seeded and finely diced
2 garlic cloves, crushed
450g/1lb mixture wild, porcini and oyster mushrooms, trimmed and sliced
1 red pepper, seeded and finely diced

2 large tomatoes, peeled and chopped
45ml/3 tbsp shoyu or soy sauce
45ml/3 tbsp vegetable stock
3 corn on the cob, boiled and kernels cut out
450g/1lb small, waxy new potatoes, boiled

Follow the instructions for making the previous mushroom mixture, then add the corn, stir thoroughly and pour into a shallow earthenware dish. Push the potatoes into the sauce and place under a hot grill until the sauce bubbles and the potatoes become crisp and lightly brown.

❧ AUTUMN SIDE DISHES ❧

❧ STUFFED MUSHROOMS ❧

4 large, flat mushrooms
basil leaves, for garnish

For the stuffing
2 large tomatoes, peeled and finely chopped

3 garlic cloves, crushed
30ml/2 tbsp olive oil
sea salt and freshly ground black pepper
45ml/3 tbsp toasted breadcrumbs

Preheat the oven to 200°C/400°F/Gas mark 6. Remove the stalks from the mushrooms. Place the stuffing ingredients in a mixing bowl and stir thoroughly. Spread the mixture over each mushroom, place on an oiled baking tray and bake for 15–20 minutes. Garnish with a few basil leaves.

❧ STICKY TOMATO TOAST ❧

4 slices wholemeal or white bread, toasted
4 or 6 tomatoes, peeled and sliced
4 garlic cloves, sliced

30ml/2 tbsp brown sugar
sea salt and freshly ground black pepper
45ml/3 tbsp olive oil

Preheat the oven to 170°C/325°F/Gas mark 3. Lightly oil a baking sheet and place the toast on it. Pour a little olive oil over each slice, then cover with tomato slices. Arrange the garlic slices in between the tomato, sprinkle with brown sugar and seasoning and dribble a little oil over the top. Bake for 2–3 hours, or until the tomato has become sticky and the bread has become crisp and caramelised.

❧ FRIED SPICY CAULIFLOWER ❧

1 cauliflower, broken into florets
60ml/4 tbsp olive oil
3 garlic cloves, sliced
1 green chilli, seeded and chopped
15ml/1 tbsp capers

12 black olives, stoned
30ml/2 tbsp nori condiment
black pepper
45ml/3 tbsp toasted breadcrumbs

Boil the cauliflower florets for 2 minutes, then drain thoroughly. In a shallow pan heat the olive oil and fry the garlic and chilli. Add the cauliflower and fry until it becomes brown and crisp. Throw in the capers and olives, then stir in the nori condiment. Add the pepper and breadcrumbs and fry until the breadcrumbs have soaked up some of the sauce and become crisp too.

❧ BROCCOLI PURÉE WITH PINE NUTS ❧

450g/1lb broccoli, trimmed and stalk peeled
30ml/2 tbsp olive oil
45ml/3 tbsp soya cream

sea salt and freshly ground black pepper
30ml/2 tbsp pine nuts, roasted

Chop the broccoli and boil for 5 minutes. Drain thoroughly, then place in a blender with the oil, cream and seasoning. Blend to a thick purée, pour into a serving dish and scatter the roasted pine nuts over the top.

Note: The quickest way of roasting seeds and nuts is to put them into a covered dry saucepan and place over the heat, shaking the pan when it gets very hot so that the contents do not burn or stick. This process should take no longer than a minute.

❈ ROASTED PARSNIPS ❈

3 or 4 parsnips, trimmed, peeled
and cut into large chunks
60ml/4 tbsp olive oil

2 garlic cloves, crushed
sea salt
lemon juice

Preheat the oven to 200°C/400°F/Gas mark 6. Boil the parsnips in salted water for about 2 minutes, then drain. Heat the oil and garlic in a baking tray, tip the parsnips into it and turn them over in the oil. Bake for 20 minutes, turn the parsnips over and return to the oven for another 20 minutes. Serve brown and crispy with sea salt and lemon juice sprinkled over them.

Note: Celeriac can be done in the same way.

❈ KOHLRABI CHIPS ❈

45ml/3 tbsp olive oil
2 or 3 kohlrabi, trimmed, peeled
and sliced into chips

sea salt
lemon juice

Heat the oil in a frying pan, throw the kohlrabi chips into it and stir-fry for 5 minutes or so until brown and cooked through. Serve sprinkled with the sea salt and lemon juice.

❈ GLAZED TURNIPS ❈

5 or 6 small turnips, trimmed,
peeled and halved

100ml/3½ fl oz sherry
45ml/3 tbsp apricot preserve

Preheat the oven to 200°C/400°F/Gas mark 6. Boil the turnips for 2 minutes, then drain thoroughly. Heat the sherry and apricot preserve in a shallow baking dish, add the turnips and make sure they are covered with the sauce. Bake for 15–20 minutes.

❋ ONION AND PARSNIP GRATIN ❋

3 or 4 parsnips, trimmed, peeled
and cut into chunks
45ml/3 tbsp olive oil
2 garlic cloves, crushed
1 green chilli, seeded and diced

2 or 3 onions, peeled and sliced
sea salt and freshly ground black
pepper
45ml/3 tbsp toasted breadcrumbs

Boil the parsnips for 2 minutes and drain thoroughly. Heat the oil in a frying pan and throw in the garlic and chilli, then the onion and parsnip. Fry for 5 minutes, or until the vegetables become crisp and brown, then season and sprinkle with the breadcrumbs. Mix thoroughly and place the pan under a hot grill until the breadcrumbs are brown.

❋ AUTUMN PUDDINGS ❋

Nigel Slater, in his marvellously inventive but practical book *Real Fast Puddings*, reminded me of what is so good about fruit crumbles: that the juice bubbles up through the crumble and makes a sticky caramelisation.* He also reminded me of how delicious chestnut purée and cooked figs can be. The following recipes attempt to reflect Slater's flair and ingenuity, but I am sure he would be appalled at the use of soya products.

* He actually says that Fay Maschler reminded him, so for once food writers are in agreement.

❋ PLUM CRUMBLE ❋

900g/2lb ripe plums, stoned
30ml/2 tbsp caster sugar
110ml/4 fl oz Marsala
110g/4oz plain flour

55g/2oz ground almonds
110g/4oz vegetable fat, preferably frozen
85g/3oz light brown sugar

Preheat the oven to 200°C/400°F/Gas mark 6. Place the plums in a pie dish, sprinkle with the caster sugar, then pour in the Marsala. To make the crumble, mix the flour, brown sugar and ground almonds together, then grate in the fat. Rub the mixture with your fingers until it resembles coarse breadcrumbs. Sprinkle in a tiny amount of cold water and stir so that some of the crumbs stick together. Scatter this mixture over the fruit and bake for about 30 minutes, or until the top is crisp and some of the juices have bubbled through.

❊ APPLE FRITTERS ❊

about 4 Bramley apples, peeled,
cored and sliced

sunflower oil for frying

For the batter
110g/4oz plain flour
55g/2oz soya flour

10ml/2 tsp baking powder
pinch of salt
30ml/2 tbsp caster sugar
pinch of cloves and cinnamon
110ml/4 fl oz soya milk
110ml/4 fl oz water
45ml/3 tbsp sunflower oil

Put the flours, baking powder, sugar and spices into a mixed bowl. Add the milk slowly, making a smooth paste, then add the water. The thinner the mixture, the lighter it will be. Beat in the oil and refrigerate for 1–2 hours. Remove from the refrigerator and beat with a fork. Drop in the apple slices. Heat a frying pan smeared with oil and fry dollops of the mixture, turning them so that they are crisp and brown on both sides. Serve with lemon slices and a little more caster sugar.

❊ STUFFED PANCAKES ❊

half quantity of batter mixture (see
Apple Fritters, above)
30ml/2 tbsp brandy or rum
6 pears, peeled, cored and sliced
5ml/1 tbsp walnut oil
45ml/3 tbsp broken walnuts

30ml/2 tbsp caster sugar
110g/4oz blueberries
110ml/4 fl oz port
60ml/4 tbsp coconut cream
violet petals, for garnish

Make the batter as in the previous recipe. Add the brandy or rum to the mixture to thin it down, and refrigerate. In a frying pan heat the walnut oil and fry the slices of pears for about 2 minutes. Sprinkle with the sugar and walnuts and continue to fry until caramelised. Add the blueberries with the port and deglaze the pan. Tip the contents into a bowl, add the coconut cream and keep warm. Make the pancakes as in the previous recipe, using enough batter to cover the bottom of the pan thinly. Allow one pancake for each person. Spoon some of the fruit mixture on to each pancake, fold the ends into the middle, sprinkle with a few violet petals and serve.

❀ CHESTNUT CREAM ❀

225g/8oz tin chestnut purée,
unsweetened
110ml/4 fl oz brandy
225g/8oz soya cream

45ml/3 tbsp icing sugar
170g/6oz dark chocolate, grated
30ml/2 tbsp flaked almonds

In a large bowl mix the chestnut purée with the brandy, add the cream and icing sugar, then stir in the grated chocolate. Toast the almonds in a dry frying pan until golden. Spoon the purée into four individual glasses and scatter the toasted almonds on top. Refrigerate for 1 hour before serving.

❀ BAKED FIGS ❀

8 ripe purple figs
55ml/2 fl oz white wine
zest and juice of 1 lemon

60ml/4 tbsp caster sugar
60ml/4 tbsp soya cream
30ml/2 tbsp flaked almonds

Preheat the oven to 200°C/400°F/Gas mark 6. Fit the figs snugly into a shallow oven dish and pour over the wine, lemon zest and juice and the sugar. Bake for 15 minutes. Baste with the juices, then pour over the cream and cook for another 5 minutes. Meanwhile, toast the almonds in a dry frying pan, until golden. Serve warm, scattered with almonds and with more cream.

❀ DAMSON CREAM ❀

700g/1lb 9oz damsons
110ml/4 fl oz dark sherry
60ml/4 tbsp maple syrup

225g/8oz tofu
225g/8oz soya cream
a few geranium petals, for garnish

Place the damsons in a pan with the sherry and maple syrup, heat gently and simmer for 10 minutes. Leave to cool, then take out all the stones and purée in a blender. Add the tofu and cream and blend until you have a thick, smooth purée. Spoon into individual glasses and refrigerate. Before serving sprinkle with a few geranium petals.

❀ CARAMEL APPLE SLICES ❀

juice of 1 lemon
8–10 eating apples, peeled, cored
and sliced

55g/2oz vegetable fat
45ml/3 tbsp caster sugar

Pour the lemon juice into a mixing bowl and tip in the apple slices, turning them so that they are covered in the juice. Melt the vegetable fat in a frying pan and lay the apple slices in it, turning them so that both sides are covered with the fat. Sprinkle over the caster sugar and leave to fry without touching until brown beneath. Place the pan under a hot grill so that the top browns and caramelises. Slip the whole lot on to a platter – they should have stuck together – and cut like a cake. Serve with soya cream.

❀ MARINATED PEACHES ❀

4–6 white, ripe peaches, peeled
and stoned
290ml/10 fl oz red wine

30ml/2 tbsp caster sugar
pinch of cloves
pinch of cinnamon

Place the peach halves flat side down in a shallow serving dish. Cover with the wine and sprinkle with the sugar and spices. Refrigerate for 2–3 days. Place under a very hot grill for 2–3 minutes, then serve.

MEALS FOR SPECIAL OCCASIONS

———

ST VALENTINE'S DINNER FOR TWO

Sorrel and Almond Soup
Wilted Salad Rossini
Moroccan Potato and Lemon Casserole with Spinach Cream
Papaya and Pomegranate Fruit Salad

SORREL AND ALMOND SOUP

225g/8oz fresh sorrel leaves
45ml/3 tbsp olive oil
85g/3oz ground almonds
620ml/22 fl oz vegetable stock

sea salt and freshly ground black pepper
110g/4oz soya cream
chopped chives, for garnish

Tear the sorrel leaves from their central spine. Heat the oil in a pan, throw in the torn leaves and cook over a gentle heat for 2–3 minutes: the sorrel immediately and very obligingly goes into a purée. Add the almonds and the stock, bring to the boil and simmer for 2–3 minutes more. Leave to cool, then blend, taste and season. Add the soya cream and reheat gently. Float a few chopped chives on the surface before serving.

WILTED SALAD ROSSINI

45ml/3 tbsp olive oil

1 Little Gem lettuce, chopped

2 small celery hearts, chopped

good pinch of salt and sugar

45ml/3 tbsp croûtons (see page 4)

6–8 dandelion leaves, chopped

few sprigs watercress, chopped

1 medium carrot, grated

4–5 black olives, stoned

little lemon juice

Heat the olive oil and throw all the chopped ingredients and the grated carrot into the pan. Add the salt and sugar. Stir-fry for a second so that the edges of the lettuce change colour but the centre does not lose its crispness. Arrange on two plates, decorate with the croûtons and olives and dribble lemon juice over the top.

MOROCCAN POTATO AND LEMON CASSEROLE

100ml/3½ fl oz olive oil

2 large onions, chopped

1 head of garlic, chopped

5ml/1 tsp ground cumin

5ml/1 tsp ground coriander

2 green chillies, seeded and chopped

900g/2lb potatoes, peeled and sliced

zest and juice of 3 lemons

860ml/1½ pints vegetable stock

sea salt

45ml/3 tbsp chopped parsley

Heat the olive oil in a large pan, throw in the onions, garlic and spices and sauté for a few minutes. Add the potatoes, lemon zest and juice, stock and salt, bring to the boil and simmer gently for 15–20 minutes. Drain off any excess liquid and reserve for soup. Place the potato mixture in a serving dish, sprinkle with the parsley and serve with spinach cream (see below).

SPINACH CREAM

225g/8oz spinach leaves, roughly chopped

45ml/3 tbsp olive oil

sea salt and freshly ground black pepper

45ml/3 tbsp soya cream

Heat the oil in a pan and throw in the spinach leaves. Season, then cover the pan and leave over a low heat for 10 minutes or until the spinach is soft. Leave to cool, then blend to a smooth purée. Add the cream and refrigerate for a few hours. Serve cold with the hot potato dish above: they make a fabulous pair.

PAPAYA AND POMEGRANATE FRUIT SALAD

2 ripe papaya

1 ripe pomegranate

55ml/2 fl oz fruit eau de vie

15ml/1 tbsp caster sugar

Cut the papaya in half and scoop out the seeds. Peel, then thinly slice the flesh into a bowl. Cut the pomegranate in half and scoop out the seeds. Scatter them over the papaya, pour the eau de vie over the top and sprinkle with caster sugar. Leave for a few hours in the refrigerator before serving.

EASTER LUNCH FOR SIX

Ribollita (Tuscan Bread Soup)
Carrot and Sherry Salad
Turkish Orange and Onion Salad
Chinese Sweet Rice Salad
Potato and Leek Strudel
Exotic Fruit Salad

RIBOLLITA (TUSCAN BREAD SOUP)

To help the ciabatta grow stale, cut the loaves into chunks when you buy them and leave in a big bowl for 3 days. (If the bread is not stale enough, it becomes slimy in the soup, which some people find unpleasant.) This is a simple dish to prepare, and everyone who tastes it loves it. In the autumn use fresh rather than tinned tomatoes, or a mixture of both.

45ml/3 tbsp olive oil
3 onions, chopped
3–4 garlic cloves, chopped
1 green chilli, seeded and finely chopped
3 × 400g/14oz tins chopped tomatoes

1.2 litres/2 pints vegetable stock
2 × 8oz tins haricot beans
2 ciabatta loaves, 3 days old
sea salt and freshly ground black pepper
handful fresh basil leaves

Heat the olive oil in a very large saucepan, throw in the onions, garlic and chilli and sauté for a minute or two. Add the tomatoes and stock, bring to the boil and simmer for another 5 minutes. Now add the beans and the bread and continue to simmer, for another 5 minutes. Taste and season. Serve with a few basil leaves scattered over the surface.

CARROT AND SHERRY SALAD

450g/1lb baby carrots, grated
1 red pepper, seeded and diced
bunch watercress, chopped

For the dressing
45ml/3 tbsp olive oil

30ml/2 tbsp dry sherry
5ml/1 tsp Dijon mustard
sea salt and freshly ground black
pepper
pinch sugar

Mix the carrots, pepper and watercress together in a large bowl. Combine all the dressing ingredients and pour over the salad. Leave to marinate for 1 hour before serving.

TURKISH ORANGE AND ONION SALAD

1 cos lettuce
4 oranges
3 red onions, peeled and cut into
rings
30ml/2 tbsp capers
75g/3oz black olives, stoned

For the dressing
zest from the 4 oranges
5ml/1 tsp white wine vinegar
5ml/1 tsp wholegrain mustard
45ml/3 tbsp olive oil
sea salt and freshly ground black
pepper
pinch sugar

Combine all the dressing ingredients in a bowl and leave for 30 minutes. On a large serving dish arrange the cos leaves in a circular pattern. Cut the remaining peel and pith away from the oranges and slice the flesh in circles. Arrange the fruit over the cos leaves, then add the onion. Scatter the capers and olives over the top and pour the dressing on to the salad just before serving.

CHINESE SWEET RICE SALAD

55g/2oz raisins
55g/2oz currants
45ml/3 tbsp soy sauce
25g/1oz ginger root, grated
small cucumber, diced
2 cloves garlic, sliced
25g/1oz pickled ginger
450g/lb cooked patna rice

45ml/3 tbsp dry sherry
15ml/1 tbsp sesame oil
30ml/2 tbsp sunflower oil
sea salt and freshly ground black
pepper
pinch sugar
110g/4oz seedless grapes
45ml/3 tbsp finely chopped green
coriander

Soak the raisins and currants in the soy sauce and sherry overnight. Heat the two oils in a wok or pan, throw in the ginger root, cucumber and garlic and fry for a moment. Add the pickled ginger, the rice, seasoning and sugar and fry for another minute. Add the dried fruit with their liquid and the grapes. Mix thoroughly and transfer to a bowl. Scatter the coriander over before serving.

POTATO AND LEEK STRUDEL

There are few chefs who create my kind of food, and none that I know of who would consider a non-dairy meal as gourmet cuisine. Anton Mossiman, however, comes close: his food is inventive, immensely tasty and very stylish. This recipe owes much to him, though he, of course, makes his own astonishingly light strudel pastry using eggs and cheese.

45ml/3 tbsp olive oil	sea salt and freshly ground black
4 medium leeks, trimmed, washed	pepper
and sliced across	5ml/1 tsp paprika
3 garlic cloves, crushed	pinch freshly grated nutmeg
1.1kg/2¼lb waxy new potatoes,	8 sheets filo pastry, thawed
boiled in their skins	a little soya milk for glazing
45ml/3 tbsp soya cream	15ml/1 tbsp sesame seeds

Preheat the oven to 200°C/400°F/Gas mark 6. Heat the olive oil in a saucepan, throw in the sliced leeks and garlic and cook over a low heat for 10–15 minutes until the leeks have softened. Slice the cooked potatoes into a large mixing bowl (there's no need to peel them), add the cooked leeks, soya cream, seasoning, paprika and nutmeg and stir thoroughly. Arrange 2 sheets of filo pastry next to each other, with their long sides just overlapping. Place 2 more sheets on top, starting 2 inches down the first sheets. Continue to layer and overlap the remaining sheets of pastry, to give a roof tile effect. Smooth the potato and leek mixture over the sheets, leaving about 10cm/4 inches around the edges. Flip these edges over so that the filling is contained. Roll the strudel up gently, like a swiss roll, shape it into a crescent and place on a greased baking tray with the joined end downwards. Brush the top and sides with soya milk, sprinkle with sesame seeds and bake for about 40 minutes until brown and crisp on the outside. Serve warm.

EXOTIC FRUIT SALAD

selection of fruit, such as papaya,
passion-fruit, rambutan, star apple,
guava, mango, mangosteen and
pineapple

caster sugar
handful flaked almonds
handful chopped dates
small glass eau de vie

Peel and chop the fruit into a huge bowl. Add a good sprinkling of caster sugar to make the juices run. Mix in the flaked almonds and dates. Pour in the eau de vie and refrigerate for 1 hour or so.

A GLYNDEBOURNE PICNIC FOR FOUR

Iced Green Pea and Courgette Soup
Stuffed Globe Artichokes
Asparagus-stuffed Croûtes
Cos and Walnut Salad
Peach Granita

ICED GREEN PEA AND COURGETTE SOUP

450g/lb fresh green peas
860ml/1½ pints vegetable stock
30ml/2 tbsp olive oil
4 medium courgettes, trimmed and sliced
2 garlic cloves, crushed

large glass dry sherry
sea salt and freshly ground black pepper
pinch sugar
few drops Tabasco (optional)

Pod the peas and boil the empty pods for 5 minutes in a little water. Pour into a blender and reduce to a pulp. Push the pulp through a sieve and reserve. Boil the peas in the vegetable stock until tender. Reserve. Heat the olive oil in a pan, throw in the courgettes and garlic and cook over a low heat for about 10 minutes until the courgettes are soft. Blend with the pod liquid. Now blend the peas and the stock and mix the two liquids together. Add the sherry, seasoning, sugar and Tabasco, if using, then refrigerate thoroughly before serving. Serve in glasses and add more sherry if you wish.

STUFFED GLOBE ARTICHOKES

4 large globe artichokes
450g/1lb broad beans, podded
zest and juice of 1 lime
2 garlic cloves, crushed

60ml/4 tbsp soya cream
sea salt and freshly ground black
pepper

Trim the artichokes by discarding the rough outer leaves and slicing the tips off the tops. Cut the bases so that they will stand upright, then place in a large saucepan, cover with water and bring to the boil. Simmer for about 40 minutes. Drain and set aside to cool. Meanwhile, boil the beans in a little water for about 4 minutes: if large, leave to cool, then slip off their outer skins. Place the beans into a blender with the lime juice and zest, the garlic and the soya cream. Blend and season. Remove the inner leaves and choke from each artichoke, leaving a solid wall of leaves on the outside. Fill the hollow with the bean purée and wrap each one individually for packing in the hamper.

ASPARAGUS-STUFFED CROÛTES

1 large baguette
450g/1lb asparagus, trimmed and
washed

30ml/2 tbsp olive oil
15ml/1 tbsp soy sauce
15ml/1 tbsp green peppercorns

Preheat the oven to 170°C/325°F/Gas mark 3. Cut the large French bread into 6cm/2½ inch slices. Cut a hollow from the centre of each slice about 1.25cm/½ inch deep, leaving a rim of about 0.5cm/¼ inch around the edge. Brush with olive oil and bake in the oven for 10 minutes or until crisp and brown. These can now be used as containers for salsas and purées.

Preheat the oven to 200°C/400°F/Gas mark 6. Place the asparagus spears in a baking dish, pour in the oil and soy sauce and roll the spears around so they are well covered. Bake for about 20 minutes until well browned and perhaps even a little crisp. Leave to cool, then chop into bite-size pieces and mix with the cooking juices and green peppercorns. Fill the croûtes with this mixture and pack securely.

COS AND WALNUT SALAD

1 large cos lettuce

55g/2oz broken walnuts

For the dressing

5ml/1 tsp lemon juice

30ml/2 tbsp walnut oil

sea salt and freshly ground black pepper

5ml/1 tsp caster sugar

5ml/1 tsp Dijon mustard

Trim and wash the lettuce and place in a large polythene bag with the broken walnuts. Mix the dressing ingredients and place in a screw-top jar. Assemble the salad just before eating. Place the leaves and nuts in a bowl, add the dressing and toss well.

PEACH GRANITA

6 large ripe peaches

zest and juice from two limes

30ml/2 tbsp maple syrup

25ml/4 fl oz dry white wine

30ml/2 tbsp slivered almonds, toasted (see page 97)

Blanch the peaches in boiling water for about 30 seconds, then skin and stone them. Put the peach flesh in a blender with the rest of the ingredients and blend briefly. The texture should be fairly coarse. Pour the mixture into a bowl and freeze for about 5 hours or overnight. Before packing the picnic hamper, take the granita out of the freezer and allow to soften for 1 hour; then break it up further and pour into a thermos. Pack the almonds separately. Serve the granita in wine glasses, sprinkled with a few roasted slivered almonds.

CHRISTMAS DINNER FOR EIGHT

Appetisers: Mushrooms Stuffed with Tapenade,
Crisp Potato Skins with Green Herb Sauce,
Dolmades of Lettuce

Cream of Sweetcorn Soup with Carrot Salsa
Cabbage, Coriander and Satay Salad
Timbale de Crêpes
Grated Brussels Sprouts with Hazelnuts
Christmas Pudding with Brandy Cream Sauce

Start the meal with some appetisers which can be served an hour or two
before dinner to keep people happy. These can all be prepared the day
before. In fact, most of the meal can be prepared in advance, leaving
you free to enjoy it with family or guests. Start the meal itself with the
soup, which is extremely easy to make and very delicious to eat. (In the
autumn I would make it with fresh corn, but frozen corn is almost as
good. Tinned corn often has added sugar, so avoid it.) Follow with the
satay salad, then the timbale de crêpes. The latter might seem involved,
but most of it can be prepared a day or even two days in advance. It is
one of my favourite festival dishes because the three different fillings
can be changed to whatever suits your palate and purse. It also looks
great when turned out and sliced like a cake. Brussels sprouts are
included simply for tradition, but they do ensure that people get their
full quota of green vitamins on the day. The Christmas pudding itself is
light but I've added both stem and crystallised ginger to it as it is one of
my favourite flavours.

APPETISERS

MUSHROOMS STUFFED WITH TAPENADE

450g/1lb small cup (not button)
mushrooms

For the tapenade
24 black olives, stoned

1 garlic clove, crushed
zest and juice of 1 lemon
45ml/3 tbsp capers
few shakes of Tabasco
olive oil

Mix all the tapenade ingredients in a blender until you have a smooth black purée. Pour into a bowl and refrigerate for 1 hour. Discard the mushroom stalks, then fill each cup to the brim with the tapenade. Refrigerate for 1 hour or serve at once.

Note: Olive pastes can be bought in most stores now, and are of good quality, but they are more expensive than making your own.

CRISP POTATO SKINS WITH GREEN HERB SAUCE

4 large potatoes, baked in their
skins and left to cool
olive oil for frying

1 large bunch basil
5ml/1 tsp sea salt
45ml/3 tbsp olive oil

For the green herb sauce
1 large bunch watercress
1 large bunch parsley
1 large bunch chives
30ml/2 tbsp Plamil egg-free
mayonnaise

Cut the potatoes in half and scoop out all the flesh, reserving it for a soup. Break up the skins and fry in hot olive oil until crisp, about 1 minute. Discard all the stalks from the herbs, then place the herbs in a blender with the salt and olive oil and reduce to a purée. Empty into a bowl and mix in the mayonnaise. Eat the crisp potato skins dipped into a little of the sauce.

DOLMADES OF LETTUCE

1 Webbs Wonder lettuce

For the stuffing
30ml/2 tbsp olive oil
2 onions, finely chopped
5 garlic cloves, finely diced
2 red peppers, seeded and diced
1 red chilli, seeded and diced

30ml/2 tbsp brown breadcrumbs
sea salt and freshly ground black pepper
5ml/1 tsp soy sauce
1 large bunch parsley, finely chopped
juice of ½ a lemon

Separate the lettuce leaves and place in a large heatproof bowl. Pour boiling water over them and drain immediately. Heat the olive oil in a large pan and throw in the onions, garlic, peppers and chilli. Cook over a high heat so that the onions and peppers slightly caramelise and blacken a tiny bit at the edges, about 2 minutes. Add the breadcrumbs and stir-fry so that the crumbs soak up the oil and juices and become a little crisp. Transfer the pan contents to a bowl, season and add the soy sauce and chopped parsley. Spread out a drained lettuce leaf, place a dessertspoonful of the mixture on a corner of the leaf and roll up, tucking the ends in as you go. If the leaf is particularly untidy, cut the edges with a knife and discard. Continue until all the mixture is used up. Arrange the dolmades on a platter and just before serving moisten with the juice of half a lemon. Young spinach leaves can be used instead of the lettuce.

CHRISTMAS DINNER

CREAM OF SWEETCORN SOUP WITH CARROT SALSA

45ml/3 tbsp olive oil
900g/2lb frozen sweetcorn,
thawed
good pinch of saffron
1.4 litres/2½ pints vegetable stock
720ml/1¼ pints soya milk
sea salt and freshly ground black
pepper
225g/8oz soya cream

For the carrot salsa
30ml/2 tbsp olive oil
2 dried chillies, broken up
2 green chillies, finely diced
2 garlic cloves, finely diced
225g/8oz carrots, trimmed and
finely diced
5ml/1 tsp caster sugar
good pinch of sea salt
5ml/1 tsp sweet paprika

Heat the olive oil in a large saucepan, throw in the sweetcorn and saffron, stir thoroughly and leave to sweat for 5 minutes. Add the vegetable stock, bring to the boil and simmer for another 5 minutes. Remove from the heat and blend in batches to a smooth, light purée. Reserve 60ml/4 tbsp of the liquid, then add the soya milk to the rest. Blend again, then season to taste and add the soya cream. Blend again. Reheat gently, without boiling, or the cream will curdle.

To make the salsa, heat the olive oil, throw in the chillies and garlic and stir for a moment. Add the diced carrots, leave to sweat for a moment, then add the reserved sweetcorn liquid. Bring to a simmer, cook gently for about 4 minutes, then stir in the sugar, salt and paprika. Place in a bowl and let people help themselves, spooning some of the salsa into the centre of the soup.

CABBAGE, CORIANDER AND SATAY SALAD

15ml/1 tbsp red wine vinegar

5ml/1 tsp maple syrup

5ml/1 tsp sea salt

15ml/1 tbsp smooth peanut butter

45ml/3 tbsp olive oil

15ml/1 tbsp coriander seeds, finely ground

2 medium onions, peeled and thinly sliced

large white cabbage

Pour the wine vinegar into a large bowl, add the maple syrup and sea salt, then work in the peanut butter. Add the oil so that you have a smooth, creamy sauce. Mix the coriander seeds into the sauce, then add the onions. Discard the outer leaves of the cabbage, then take out the white core using a sharp knife. Grate the leaves into the sauce and toss well. Leave for 10 minutes before serving.

TIMBALE DE CRÊPES

This dish consists of pancakes interleaved with various purées and vegetables and cooked in a soufflé dish. Everything can be cooked the day before, even the crêpes, if you interleave them with greaseproof paper. The finished dish can be assembled on the day itself. The quantities below make 10–12 crêpes for a 23cm/9 inch soufflé dish.

For the crêpes
110g/4oz wholewheat flour
55g/2oz soya flour
10ml/2 tsp baking powder
good pinch of salt
110ml/4 fl oz soya milk
15ml/1 tbsp oregano
110ml/4 fl oz water
few drops Tabasco
45ml/3 tbsp olive oil

For the leek and tofu custard
45ml/3 tbsp olive oil
450g/1lb leeks, trimmed, washed and sliced across
sea salt and freshly ground black pepper
225g/8oz tofu, broken up

For the sweet potato and tempeh filling
45ml/3 tbsp olive oil
2 onions, peeled and sliced
3 garlic cloves, chopped
1 green chilli, seeded and diced

2 large sweet potatoes, peeled and cut into chunks
225g/8oz tempeh, thawed and cut into chunks
sea salt and freshly ground black pepper

For the oyster and porcini mushroom cream sauce
45ml/3 tbsp olive oil
225g/8oz oyster mushrooms, washed and sliced
110g/4oz porcini, soaked in dry sherry for 1 hour
45ml/3 tbsp soya cream
sea salt and freshly ground black pepper

For the green pepper and sage sauce
45ml/3 tbsp olive oil
6 green peppers, seeded and sliced
sea salt and freshly ground black pepper
handful fresh sage leaves, well chopped

Make the crêpe batter at least 24 hours before needed. It is all the better for resting. Mix the flours, baking powder, salt and oregano in a bowl, add the milk bit by bit, stirring all the time to make a smooth paste. Beat in the water, using an electric mixer, then add the Tabasco and oil. Cover and refrigerate for 24 hours. Before using, beat it vigorously again. Smear a frying pan with a little oil or grease, then ladle in enough batter to cover the pan and make a crêpe roughly the size of the soufflé dish. If the mixture is too thick, add a little more water to the batter. It doesn't matter if the first crêpe is a little thick as it will be used as a base. When the crêpe begins to dry out on top, flip it over and cook briefly on the other side. Pile up the cooked crêpes, interleaving them with greaseproof paper.

To make the leek and tofu custard, heat the olive oil in a pan, throw in the leeks with the seasoning and leave to sweat with the lid on for about 5 minutes. Add the tofu and cook for another 3 minutes. Reserve.

To make the sweet potato and tempeh filling, heat the oil in a strong, thick-bottomed pan, throw in the onions, garlic and chilli and leave to cook for a moment. Add the sweet potato, stir thoroughly, then cover the pan and cook gently for 15 minutes. Add the tempeh, mix thoroughly and cook for another 10 minutes. Season and reserve.

To make the mushroom cream sauce, heat the olive oil and cook both kinds of mushrooms with the sherry in a covered pan until soft, about 3 minutes. Blend roughly, adding the cream and seasoning, and reserve.

To make the pepper and sage sauce, heat the olive oil, throw in the remaining ingredients, then cover the pan and cook gently for 20 minutes. Leave to cool, then blend to make a thick, smooth green sauce. Reserve.

To assemble the Timbale

Preheat the oven to 200°C/400°F/Gas mark 6. Grease the soufflé dish, then arrange four crêpes around the sides, allowing 2.5cm/1 inch at the bottom and as much as possible to overlap at the top. Place one crêpe in the bottom of the dish and cover with the mushroom cream sauce. Place another crêpe over it and pour in the leek and tofu custard. Place a crêpe over that and top with the sweet potato and tempeh. When the soufflé dish is full, fold the overlapping edges of the crêpes in the middle and cover with another crêpe. Place a piece of foil over the dish, sit it in a baking tin filled with boiling water and place in the preheated oven for 1 hour. Remove the timbale from the oven, leave to rest for 10 minutes or more, then unmould on to a large platter. Pour the Green Pepper and Sage Sauce over the top and surround with watercress sprigs. Serve with the grated Brussels sprouts and a green leaf salad.

GRATED BRUSSELS SPROUTS WITH HAZELNUTS

1kg/2lb 2oz Brussels sprouts, trimmed

30ml/2 tbsp hazelnut oil

sea salt and freshly ground black pepper

55g/2oz hazelnuts, roughly ground

Feed all the sprouts into a grating disc on a food processor. Heat the hazelnut oil in a large pan, throw in the grated sprouts with the seasoning, then stir and cook for about 3 minutes. They should reduce their bulk by two-thirds. Serve the sprouts with the ground nuts sprinkled over them.

CHRISTMAS PUDDING WITH BRANDY CREAM SAUCE

110g/4oz currants

110g/4oz sultanas

110g/4oz raisins

110g/4oz mixed peel

110g/4oz crystallised ginger

110g/4oz stem ginger, chopped

60ml/4 tbsp stem ginger juice

110g/4oz muscovado sugar

5ml/1 tsp grated nutmeg

55g/2oz flaked almonds

170g/6oz wholemeal breadcrumbs

55g/2oz wholemeal flour

225g/8oz vegetable suet

juice and zest of 2 oranges

45ml/3 tbsp rose water

110ml/4 fl oz dark rum

For the brandy cream sauce

225g/8oz tofu

60ml/4 tbsp maple syrup

60ml/4 tbsp brandy

225g/8oz soya cream

Mix together all the pudding ingredients in a large bowl, cover with a clean tea towel and leave to sit for 1 day. Grease a 3 pint pudding basin and pack the mixture in. Cover with greased greaseproof paper, aluminium foil and a cloth and steam for 8 hours. Steam for another 2 hours before eating the pudding on Christmas Day.

To make the brandy sauce, mix all the ingredients in a blender until you have a smooth pouring sauce.

APPENDICES

THE PREJUDICES

Distrust and disdain for the plant diet is embedded in prejudices that go deep within the psyche of Western people. It is not simply that it is frowned on by the food élite, not simply this tacit understanding that plant food cannot be a cuisine in itself to inspire respect. (A strange anomaly, the latter, for respect is given to the great dishes of southern India, which are almost animal-free except for their use of yoghurt.) Respect is given to many individual ethnic dishes worldwide, but not to plant cuisine as a whole.

No, the reasons for the disdain are built on several factors. It is due partly to the fact that asceticism has never been extolled as admirable, wise or even stylish, in Western culture as it has been in nearly all Eastern cultures. Here in the West, asceticism has come under the curse of Christendom, which removes all the joy from self-sacrifice and turns it into punishment. Even the term 'self-sacrifice' suggests something one misses badly, when in truth it is something one gives up gladly. So asceticism has traditionally been seen as a form of self-martyrdom, self-denigration, a total abnegation of pleasure, a form of freaky masochism. Those adopting it are considered fools when they could be indulging themselves in all the great flavours and delicacies on offer. Yet Epicurus,[1] who gave his name to feasts of splendour, knew that true pleasure stemmed from selection – that the pleasure was all the keener for what was omitted, for the senses were heightened to appreciate the little that was left. True Epicurean philosophy has failed to permeate our Western culture; the very term has become a travesty of the original concept.

Within the disdain of plant food sceptics I have also detected an underlying fear which, I believe, springs from the race memory: that surviving on much less food is tantamount to the onset of famine. We must not forget that we have only to go back a mere ten generations to reach a time when, especially in the winter months, food was at subsistence level – if one was lucky. Each day was spent hungry, and getting anything to eat occupied the whole of the mind and being. In fact, we do not have to go far back in time to find evidence of food shortage: many of us have grandparents who suffered from malnutrition. Medical recruiting officers in the First World War were horrified to discover so many underweight adult men of low stature and in parlous health. In many parts of the modern world, famine is still with us. It is perhaps not too excessive to point out that the spectre of famine haunts the overladen Western table groaning under the surfeit of food from all parts of the world. We know, somewhere within us, that this is a daily obscenity that we choose to live with.

THE REALITIES

It has now become almost a truism that the diet of the affluent West is a killer. The high amount of saturated fats in animal flesh and dairy produce clogs up arteries, promotes obesity and has produced an epidemic of coronary disease. Recent scientific research in the United States found that those who eat red meat on a daily basis are two and a half times more likely to develop colon cancer.[2] An epic study in China found that lowering fat consumption to 15 per cent of calories prevents most diseases of affluence from developing. Chinese villagers on low-fat, low-meat diets also suffered less anaemia and osteoporosis than their urban counterparts eating more meat. Yet both of these conditions are still commonly thought of as being caused by a diet too low in protein. Professor Colin Campbell, one of the leaders of the China study, told the *New York Times*: 'We're basically a vegetarian species and should be eating a wide variety of plant foods and minimising our intake of animal foods.'[3]

Yet governments continue to subsidise the meat and dairy industries with taxpayers' money (the surplus milk lake and beef mountain cost us many billions alone), while the taxpayers themselves continue to consume the very foods that make them terminally ill. Such a situation is truly lunatic, yet it is accepted with little comment. Vested interests in the products from exploited animals place persistent and steady pressure upon society to continue to consume them, in some cases under the guise of health (see pages 121–3). The public is understandably confused as experts often change their minds on what constitutes healthy eating. For the last thirty years, however, experts have never deviated from the simple and obvious belief that saturated fat is the main cause of heart disease.

The ecological destruction of our planet by the rearing and slaughter each year of 15 billion livestock is an increasingly urgent problem that governments refuse to face. Certain countries, such as The Netherlands, are unable to cope adequately with the pollution from their dairy herds, so EU rulings designate them 'manure-surplus areas'. They now have so much animal excrement that they dry it and export it by sea to India. This, however, does not solve the whole problem: residual ammonia poisons the land and water, causing heather and lilies to wilt in nature reserves. In an effort to overcome this, indoor animal farms have installed ammonia traps.

What is more, meat-eating around the world is on the increase, as newly affluent countries with their oil riches spend more on élitist food. (Traditionally, vegetables have always been related to poverty and meat to riches.) Even with intensive modern farming, there can never be enough meat for everyone as there is not enough grain available to feed the livestock. To support the world's current population of 5.4 billion on an American-style diet, which includes 225g/8oz of grain-fed meat per day, would require two and a half times as much grain as the world's farmers produce for all purposes. At the moment we all subsidise meat-eaters. The price of meat would quadruple if the full ecological costs – fossil fuel combustion, groundwater depletion, agricultural and chemical pollution, methane and ammonia emission – were included in the bill.

Another great problem is what to do with surplus fat production in a society which is becoming increasingly health conscious and demanding low-fat products. Governments show an almost cynical disregard for the life and health of their citizens when you consider that much of the surplus fat produced by dairy herds is given almost free to schoolchildren, to the poor and the infirm in hospitals or to poorer nations. In eastern Europe, where the EU has disposed of surplus butterfat for the last three decades, coronary heart disease has doubled. In the United States it has been estimated that if everyone cut their fat intake to the recommended maximum it would cut meat consumption by up to 40 per cent.

What we eat has a direct effect upon our environment. Cattle, for example, play a prominent role in global desertification. Livestock are also a source of the second most important greenhouse gas, methane. They account for 15–20 per cent of global methane emissions – about 3 per cent of global warming from all gases. Our present diet depletes the world's seas of fish and pollutes their habitat, while our reliance on meat and chemically grown fruit and vegetables pollutes the soil, making it more and more arid and infertile. With an ever-growing world population putting excessive demands on our food supply, you might suppose that this is inevitable. The answer is an unequivocal no. 'Plant-centred diets, such as those consumed around the Mediterranean Sea during the 1950s and 1960s, would be environmentally beneficial because they imply need for a much smaller population of domestic animals and, consequently, lowered demand on soil, water and energy resources.'[4] Thus, if society as a whole cut down its meat consumption by two-thirds, we could restore livestock production to its historical role, where the animals' presence was part of the beneficial life-cycle of the land, returning nutrients to the soil as manure.

THE HISTORY

In order to see more clearly the rights and wrongs within the nature of our food today, it helps to put it within a historical context.

MEAT-EATING IN THE PAST

We hear so much about 'traditional foods' and what people ate in the past, yet too often this information is fudged or distorted out of ignorance. For example, we hear a great deal about Britain being a meat-eating nation, but that was true only of the aristocracy and the wealthy. From the end of the Roman occupation to the nineteenth century the majority of people ate meat maybe only twice or three times a year, at the major festivals of Easter, Michaelmas and Christmas. If they were lucky, they slaughtered their only pig in November, salted and preserved it so that it would last throughout the winter, using a little of the meat to flavour the everyday fare of vegetable stews or pottages, which were thickened with cereals and pulses. This was single-pot cooking over a low fire, and the pot simmered throughout the day. The greens used were brassicas, such as cabbage and kale, which would have given out their distinctive sulphurous aroma, but wild herbs and greens were also used, as well as dried beans and peas, which counted as the main protein of the meal.

The nineteenth-century German socialist Friedrich Engels used the amount of meat eaten in a family as a guide to their income. Among the Irish, the very poor, the diet consisted only of potatoes with no meat at all; next to them came families who ate bread, cheese, porridge and potatoes, but still no meat; then came families who could afford a small piece of bacon, finely chopped, to flavour the potatoes on one day of the week. Among the working classes a family counted as doing well if they ate a small piece of meat two or three times a week. The sign of real status was when you could afford to put meat on the table every day of the week.

Thus, Britain was hardly a meat-eating nation – more like a meat-eating upper class. Also, we rarely hear the fact (and if we do, it is not related to diet in any way) that this small section of society tended to be obese and to suffer from rheumatism, gout, heart disease and other illnesses. The great period of consuming meat – the eighteenth century, when the essayist Sydney Smith said he had eaten 44 wagon-loads of it during his life – was also a century well known for obesity, gout and rheumatism. All this, despite the fact that animal carcasses in the past were far lower in saturated fats than they are now. Before the Enclosures Acts in the eighteenth century, domestic livestock still closely resembled their wild ancestors: the medieval pig, for example, looked like a wild boar. Wild animals have only 3–4 per cent fat on them, which tends to be polyunsaturated, while modern animals can have 25 per cent or more saturated fat. In the past animal fat was used in tallow-making to light dwellings and was not consumed. The advent of gas lighting closely followed by electricity meant that carcass fat began to be used in food processing and preparation. These are the hidden fats which are now such a cause for concern and in which all convenience foods are so high.

The beginnings of food technology occurred around the same time as the advent of gas and electric lighting: canning, freezing, self-raising flour and baking powder, packet gelatine and blancmange powder, sweetened condensed milk, margarine and commercially bottled pickles, sauces and soups all appeared in the last quarter of the nineteenth century and successfully released the household cook from the chore of turning a product straight from the fields into an appetising meal. Good cooking, as stated earlier, has its source in a close and creative relationship between the land and the kitchen. Unfortunately, this tie has been severed and in the Western world there seems little hope that it can be fully recovered. Only those single-minded people who tend their own gardens and resolutely refuse to buy anything else can be said to carry on the tradition. Others can compromise by buying locally produced organic vegetables. In this way the relationship with the land can draw closer.

MILK CONSUMPTION IN THE PAST

Consumption of dairy products must have developed soon after the domestication of animals around 13,000 BC. Cows were kept as draught animals, so fresh milk came from sheep and goats. The milk was squeezed into a container made from either a calf's stomach or bladder, and this would have immediately soured it for cheese-making. What was drunk was the whey left after the curds congealed. In Roman times cows' milk was still frowned upon as a drink in itself. Virgil makes the point that cows' milk is for calves, not humans. All through the Middle Ages cows' milk was turned into cheese, while its by-product, whey, was drunk. The milk products – butter, cream, cheese, buttermilk – were far more valuable to the farmer as saleable products than the milk itself. The idea that a farmer's family would have drunk copious amounts of fresh milk is absurd, for as we know, milk turns very quickly, especially in the summer months and in the unhygienic conditions that existed in the past. Perhaps that is why the nobility believed milk was bad for the health: they claimed it curdled in the stomach and would not touch it. Much more popular were drinks made with milk curdled by ale – so-called possets. These were often flavoured with spices, fruits and honey, then strained and made into a dessert which would be cut into slices.

What is interesting about this is that recent research into dairy fats has led nutritionists to believe that when cheese or yoghurt are consumed, they do not have the deleterious effect upon the arteries which milk itself has. This is because the process of curdling changes the molecular structure of the fats and something less harmful is created. The idea that milk is a healthy food is, in fact very recent indeed. It goes back to the 1920s when a child expert called Trudy King recommended cows' milk as a good substitute for mother's milk. It's not. Each species produces the milk that its infants need to grow. Cows' milk is composed of nutrients to build strong bones and large bodies. Consumption of milk is the main factor behind the rise in body weight and height of people living in the affluent West, and also accounts for the postwar growth in body size of the Japanese. Mother's milk is composed of fatty acids, Omega 3 and Omega 6, in a one to one ratio. These are specifically designed for neural growth, the expansion of brain tissue and the nervous system. Mother's milk is essential for the intelligence of the child. Similarly, the food we need to consume is that which promotes and stimulates brain tissue, for we need intelligence, not big bones. The world's future lies in acknowledging this and making sure the human race consumes the right food.[5]

NUTRITION – SOME MYTHS, ASSUMPTIONS AND FACTS

There are numerous myths and assumptions about the plant diet. For example, some people worry about the nutritional content of a diet that omits some foods latterly thought to be vital to health. This is a terrible misapprehension.

The high consumption of milk and animal fats has been linked closely not only with the rising incidence of coronary heart disease, but also with osteoporosis. New Zealand and the United States, the two countries with the highest milk consumption in the world, also have the highest incidence of osteoporosis. This fact should scotch forever the myth that dairy products are necessary for a daily intake of calcium. Hip fracture rates in Europe show that Norway, with the highest milk consumption, is far in the lead, while the UK is not far behind. Research from 1977 to 1987 in Greece, where the consumption of milk products from 1960 to 1990 nearly doubled, showed that hip fracture rates increased by 50 per cent.[6] The rise in these countries is as much due to increased animal protein in the diet as it is to milk consumption because animal protein increases the excretion of calcium in the urine.

On the other hand, studies in Mediterranean countries and Asia show the benefits of a plant-based diet. These places all 'exhibit low rates of many chronic diseases and long life expectancies. A high consumption of plant foods confers numerous health benefits; investigations support links between increased vegetable, fruit and fibre consumption and lower rates of several cancers, coronary heart disease, neural tube defects and cataracts.'[7]

There have also been numerous studies which indicate that a plant diet has beneficial effects almost immediately upon people suffering from high blood pressure and angina, kidney disease (too much protein impairs kidney function), rheumatoid arthritis, atherosclerosis and even asthma.[8] An aspect which must help the health of both vegans and vegetarians is that they are lighter in weight than the average omnivore. This is mainly because animal protein is associated with saturated fat, which can lead to obesity, while plant protein contains fibre.

'A substantial amount of epidemiological and clinical data indicates that a high intake of plant foods and complex carbohydrates is associated with a reduced risk of several chronic diseases, especially coronary heart disease, certain cancers, hypertension and diabetes.'[9]

'A varied wholefood vegan diet contains adequate levels of energy and protein to sustain good health in all age groups as evidenced in studies of vegans across the world.'[10]

VITAMIN B$_{12}$

Another inevitable reaction to the news of my current diet is: but surely you have to take vitamin supplements? When told that people like myself possibly acquire a better range of vitamins and minerals than omnivores because our consumption of fresh fruit and vegetables is that much higher, the reaction is disbelief and usually concludes with a triumphant: 'Ah, but you have to take vitamin B$_{12}$, surely?'

No, we don't. The so-called vitamin B$_{12}$ deficiency to which vegans are vulnerable is an obsession in the nutritional world, so much so that one is inclined to think it is a subconscious form of 'vegan bashing' – a method by which 'nutritionists' can dismiss the whole diet and its philosophy as unsound. Let us look at the facts.

The first obvious signs of B$_{12}$ deficiency is pins and needles or coldness in hands and feet, fatigue and weakness, poor concentration and even psychosis. But a B$_{12}$ deficiency is extremely rare, so rare in fact that every case gets written up, which makes it seem more common than it is. The amount of vitamin B$_{12}$ we all need is infinitesimal. A whole lifetime's requirement of B$_{12}$ 'adds up to a 40-milligram speck of red crystals – about one seventh the size of an average tablet of aspirin.'[11]

B$_{12}$ is stored in the liver, which usually contains enough for a period of 3–6 years. The vitamin is produced by bacteria which live in the soil and in the intestines of humans and other animals. Our bodies have ways of conserving B$_{12}$ by recycling it from bile, decreasing the loss from the kidneys and increasing its rate of absorption from food. Some individuals, it is now thought, have bacteria present in the small intestine which manufacture B$_{12}$ and make it available to the body.

So where do omnivores get their B$_{12}$? They get it from meat and dairy products, as long as the food is not cooked thoroughly. B$_{12}$ is destroyed by high temperatures, so it is absent in boiled milk and well-roasted meat. Animals top up their B$_{12}$ by eating grass and herbage which have bacteria on them. Vegans too can get a good supply of B$_{12}$ from eating organically grown vegetables which have not been *too* thoroughly washed. If vegans are still concerned that they may not be acquiring enough of this vitamin, they can turn to yeast extracts and fortified margarines, soya milk, soya mince and chunks (check the labels of all these items for the B_{12} content), nutritional yeast, sourdough bread and shiitake mushrooms.

Until recently it was thought that seaweeds, tempeh, soy sauce, miso and tofu were also good sources of B_{12}, but it now seems that what they have are chemical analogues which may block the digestion of the tiny amount of real B_{12} they also contain.

There have been several research studies on B_{12} intake in groups of vegans worldwide over the last thirty years. Many of these groups took no vitamin supplements and had no deficiency. It was found that when there was no B_{12} available in the diet and no supplements or fortified foods were taken, the serum levels of B_{12} generally fell after a number of years, but they often stabilised at a low yet still useful figure. Vegans of twenty to thirty-five years' standing have only very rarely been found to show clinical symptoms of the deficiency. Most cases of deficiency occur in omnivores who lack the intrinsic factor required for absorption of B_{12}.[12]

B_{12} is now added to bread and flour, so even if all the above was not true, people on a plant diet would still be getting plenty, if not far too much, of this vitamin in their daily diet.

THE POLITICS

Throughout history food has always been used as a weapon of political domination. The power nexus which controls the food supply controls the will of the people. It is as simple as that.

Things are no different today. In a world market economy the will of the people has to be guided to buy the foods which the power nexus wishes us to buy. Television advertising is a powerful and persuasive Big Brother, indoctrinating 90 per cent of our society into buying foods which, in the long run, destroy the health of the whole community. If you do not believe me, watch the TV advertisements throughout one evening and count up the number of foods advertised which are based on high quantities of animal fats, sugars and salt. You will discover that other foods (the healthy ones alluded to in this book) are never advertised at all. Why? Because there is no profit in their sale for the food manufacturers. Profits lie only in the high-fat, highly refined foods. The public are being conned. What is more, they seem happy to be conned and not to ask any awkward questions.

The fewer the questions asked about the realities behind our food supply, the happier the suppliers, for food today is a very dirty business. But because we live in a market economy, the power of controlling the food supply lies with the consumers. This is the first time historically this has happened: consumers can change the world market, completely revolutionise it, if they want to. They could start insisting that they eat only healthy foods, insist that animals are not reared for the table, insist that food is not imported from 10,000 miles away, insist that local farmers stop using pesticides and fertilisers on their soil . . . All they have to do is to make their voices heard. This can be done by boycotting all the wrong, unhealthy foods and buying only the others. In a very small way this has already begun to happen.[13] What we now need is a mass protest against the exploitation of animals and the pollution of our planet. We can stop it, and it begins with what we choose to eat.

THE FUTURE

Without any consumer action the future, as seen by market analysts, is a bleak one. By the year 2000 it has been estimated that 90 per cent of our food will be convenience articles, packaged, refined and ready for consumption in a matter of seconds.[14] This will leave a huge majority of the population without any culinary skills whatsoever. I see an ever greater polarisation within society, where a section of the community revolts from this picture and either grows its own produce, or takes care to select it from a more personal source, and then takes pride in cooking it. There is now a growing demand for organic vegetables which can be delivered weekly.[15]

I fear that manufactured food will grow ever more fatty unless the vast dairy herds decline in number. This will happen only if the public stop buying dairy produce in the amounts they do now because they realise how adversely it is affecting their health. Public perception still sees milk as healthy, and until the media (the greatest influence upon the public) takes this on board little will change.

Notes

1 Greek philosopher who lived 341–270 BC and taught that pleasure was the beginning and end of life. He advised avoiding those foods which, though giving pleasure at the time, afterwards leave one feeling deprived.
2 Worldwatch Paper 103: *Taking Stock: Animal Farming and the Environment*, Alan B. Durning and Holly B. Brough, Washington, 1991.
3 Ibid.
4 *Mediterranean Diets: Are They Environmentally Responsible?*, Joan Dye Gussow, *Supplement to the American Journal of Clinical Nutrition*, Vol 61, June 1995.
5 See *The Driving Force*, Michael Crawford & David Marsh, Heinemann, London, 1989.
6 *Health Implications of Mediterranean Diets in Light of Contemporary Knowledge. 1 Plant Foods and Dairy Products*, Laurence H. Kushi, Elizabeth B. Lenart & Walter C. Willett, *Supplement to the American Journal of Clinical Nutrition*, Vol 61, June 1995.
7 Ibid.
8 *Vegan Nutrition – A Survey of Research*, Gill Langley, *The Vegan Society*, London, 1995.
9 *Report on Diet, Nutrition and the Prevention of Chronic Diseases*, The World Health Organisation, 1990.
10 Gill Langley, ibid.
11 Ibid.
12 Ibid.
13 *The Unmanageable Consumer*, Yiannis Gabriel & Tim Lang, Sage Publications Ltd, London, 1995.
14 *The Food System*, Geoff Tansy & Tony Worsley, Earthscan, London, 1995.
15 Contact the Soil Association which has a list. Their address is 86, Colston St, Bristol, BS1 5BB. Tel: 0117 9290061.

INDEX